AROUND TOKYO

TOKYO

A Day-Tripper's Guide

by John Turrent
Jonathan Lloyd-Owen

The **Japan Times**, Ltd.

First edition: January, 1982
Second printing: May, 1982
Jacket design by Tsutomu Nakagawa

Published by The Japan Times, Ltd.
5-4, Shibaura 4-chome, Minato-ku, Tokyo 108, Japan
ISBN4-7890-0163-6

Printed in Japan

FOREWORD

This book is a collection of articles adapted from the Weekend Leisure Guide column carried in The Japan Times over the past three years. It aims to provide information on leisure spots in and around Tokyo which are less well-known to foreign residents and visitors — and sometimes to Japanese people as well.

The articles, while not meant to provide a comprehensive guide to the area, have been selected in order to show the great variety of places worth visiting around Tokyo and to give foreigners the opportunity to branch away from established tourist courses and enjoy the kind of day trips which Japanese themselves make. It is hoped that by using this book readers will be able to experience a variety of aspects of Tokyo — and Japanese — life and culture on a relatively cheap budget.

There is one trip described in the book which cannot be undertaken in a single day — that to the distant Ogasawara Islands. However, this was included in order to emphasize, again, the great variety of trips possible within Tokyo's boundaries. All other excursions can easily be made in one day and are recommended for weekend outings, and even more so for weekday outings when places are usually less crowded.

We would like to express our special thanks to Ms. Naoko Nakamura for allowing us to include her article on Mother Farm, and to Ms. Ina Krantz for her constant editorial assistance. We would also like to thank the Japan National Tourist Organization for their regular supply of information which enabled us to include a monthly calendar of events.

January, 1982
John Turrent
Jonathan Lloyd-Owen

CONTENTS

Parks and Gardens

Koishikawa Korakuen   2
Mukojima Hyakkaen   4
Tetsugakudo Park   6
Rikugien   8
Arisugawa Memorial Park   10
Sankeien   12
Cycling Parks   14
Boating Lakes   16
Kannonzaki Park   18
Oi Bird Park   20

Museum Parks

Roka Park   24
Earthquake Memorial Museum   26
Nihon Minkaen   28
Okamoto Minkaen   31
Koganei Park   33
Machida Iseki Park   35
Kasori Shell Mound   37
Ome Railway Park   39
Mikasa Park   42
UNESCO Village   44
Hakone Open Air Museum   46

Zoos, Farms and Leisure Grounds

Ueno Zoo 50
Mother Farm 52
Children's Zoos 54
Tobu Zoological Park 56
Leisure Grounds 58

Temples, Shrines and Cathedrals

Kuhonbutsu 62
Hikawa Shrine 64
Heirinji 66
Cathedrals 68

Historical Routes

Arakawa Line Tram 72
Yokohama I 74
Yokohama II 77
Kamakura 80
Ichikawa 83
Odawara 85

Rivers, Caves and Mountains

Sumida River 88
Kanda River 90
Nagatoro 93
Yoshimi Caves 95
Taya Caves 97
Mt. Takao 99
Mt. Fuji 101

Seashores and Islands

Fujisawa 104
Aburatsubo 106

Enoshima 108
Ogasawara Islands 110

Fairs and Markets

Antique Fairs 114
Tsukiji Fish Market 116

Museums and Archives

Michio Miyagi Memorial Hall 120
Kite Museum 122
Daimyo Clock Museum 124
Shitamachi Museum 126
Yokohama Archives 128
List of Museums 130

Tokyo From Above

Skyscrapers 134
Light Plane 137

Calendar

Month by Month 140

Area Maps

152

Parks and Gardens

Mukojima Hyakkaen

Stroll in the Original Korakuen

Koishikawa Korakuen　　　　　　　　　　　小石川後楽園

The area known as Korakuen in Tokyo's Bunkyo Ward is famous as a sports and amusement center. A constant stream of people flows to and from the baseball stadium, recreation park and bowling alley in an atmosphere of busy and noisy entertainment.

To the west of the stadium and in stark contrast to its neighboring empire of fun is located the original Korakuen, a landscaped garden offering numerous picturesque scenes and a peaceful mood. The garden is called Koishikawa Korakuen, built in the 17th century and carefully preserved from the encroachments of the surrounding city environment.

Construction of the garden was begun in 1629 by Tokugawa Yorifusa (1603-61) and continued by his son Mitsukuni (1628-1700) until it was completed 30 years later. Mitsukuni had a great attachment through study to China and Confucianism and he invited to Japan the Chinese scholar Chu Shun-shui (1600-82), a refugee from the Ming Dynasty. It was Chu Shun-shui who helped in the design of the garden and introduced a strong Chinese tone to it.

It was Chu Shun-shui also who gave the garden its name. He wasn't to know that the name would become sweepingly associated with the world of baseball, but *"koraku"* was taken from a Confucian saying, and carries the meaning that "a sage must be first to endure and overcome hardships in order to bring happiness to the people, and be the last to share in that happiness."

Koishikawa Korakuen is known as a stroll park, and indeed during the stroll there are several ideal places at which to stop and take in the beauty of scenic spots in China and Japan which have

2

been reproduced here. The places to note are many, among them the miniature copy of the dyke of Sai-ko, West Lake in China; the Shiraito no Taki, a waterfall so called because it resembles a screen of white threads; a small hill modeled after Loshan in China; the Kuhachiya sake house, which looks as if it must have been a very merry and intimate drinking place in Edo days, and the Tokujindo shrine, built in 1630 and the oldest building in the garden.

One pleasure about the stroll around the garden is the number of bridges. There is something special about any kind of bridge, connecting one scene with another, and Koishikawa Korakuen has a variety. They range from the Togetsu-kyo, a replica of a bridge in Kyoto, which crosses over a river literally jammed with carp of all colors and sizes, to the red, antique-like Tsuken-kyo bridge, a copy of the bridge in the precincts of Tofukuji Temple in Kyoto.

On a more simple level there is the Yatsu-hashi bridge, built of eight zigzag planks, and even simpler is the Sawatari, stepping stones across the stream. One of the most striking sights in the garden is the Engetsu-kyo, a stone bridge so called because a full moon is formed by the arch of the bridge and its reflection in the water.

As well as the bridges, another intriguing feature of the garden is the number of stones and rocks found here and there, each with a fascinating shape, from the mildly erotic "male" and "female" stones, the screen rock, the natural stone with a hollow, to the Tokudaiji-seki, the great stone facing the lakelet. There are also a number of stone lanterns and monuments.

The garden is open from 9 a.m. to 4:30 p.m., closed on Mondays, and there is an entrance fee of ¥200.

The best approach to Korakuen is from Iidabashi Station on the JNR Sobu Line, from where it is a 10-minute walk.

Garden of a Hundred Flowers

Mukojima Hyakkaen   向島百花園

Sawara Kiku-u was born in Sendai in 1766 and moved to Edo (Tokyo) in the 1780s where he later opened an antique curio shop in Nihonbashi. This he managed for some 10 years before buying a plot of land in Mukojima on the east bank of the Sumida River. He had by this time entered the circles of the Edo literary world and counted among his friends the scholar Murata Harumi (1747-1881); the humorist Ota Nanpo (1749-1823); the Confucian scholar Kameda Hosai (1752-1826), and Okubo Shibutsu, the poet (1767-1837). It was from these friends that he received 360 plum trees, which formed the beginning in 1804 of Mukojima Hyakkaen.

It was these friends who also helped Kiku-u to lay out the garden, its paths, the pond and the general countryside setting. Flowers for all seasons and from all places were brought here and the name gradually stuck — Garden of a Hundred Flowers. During the Tokugawa Period it became the meeting place for writers, poets and artists as well as a regular destination for Edo day-trippers.

Kiku-u died in 1831 and after that the garden passed through several hands. As the original circle of friends passed away, the garden began to lose much of its attraction until it caught the attention of a businessman, Tsunekichi Ogura (1865-1934), who restored it and reopened it to the public. After his death the garden was handed over to the Tokyo authorities by his widow in 1938 to preserve it forever as a scenic spot.

The garden itself occupies only a small area but is full of flowers ranging from modest forsythia, peonies and morning glories to the more spectacular displays of plum and cherry blossoms and irises. Dotted about the garden, usually in the shade of the trees, are large

4

stone monuments inscribed with *haiku* verse, including some by the famous poet Matsuo Basho.

Hyakkaen is actually one stop on the Sumida River course tracing the Seven Gods of Luck. The artists who helped Kiku-u to set up the garden hunted out the seven deities in the temples and shrines in the area, starting with the God of Wealth and Longevity (Fukurokuji) which Kiku-u possessed. With a map guiding the way at each stop, they now form a pleasant tour of the east bank of the river, taking in also Sumida Park and a "transport park" on the way.

To name the spots briefly, they begin with Mimeguri Shrine, famous for the stone monument carrying the *haiku* verse of Enomoto Kikaku (1661-1717), who, it is said, passed by here in 1693 during a long drought in Edo and on seeing villagers gathered to pray for rain, wrote the verse in honor of them. The next day it rained. This shrine is dedicated to the gods of Wealth and Fortune (Ebisu and Daikoku). The next stop north is Kofukuji Temple, said to have been first built in 1673 and dedicated to the God of Fortune (Hotei). With its Chinese-style main gateway, this multistoried structure is said to be one of the finest of its kind in Tokyo.

Proceeding north, the next stop is Chomeiji Temple, originally built in 1615 and dedicated to Benzaiten. In the Edo Period this temple was a popular spot for snow-viewing and there is a monument of Basho's snow *haiku* verse here. Shirahige Shrine is said to have been originally built in 951. The present structure was built in 1864 and is one of the oldest buildings in the area. This shrine, the nearest to Hyakkaen, is dedicated to the God of Longevity (Jurojin). Furthest north is Tamonji Temple, offering a rustic appearance with its thatched gateway and dedicated to the God of Treasure (Bishamonten).

Although the area has changed much in appearance as a result of the high-rise expressways sweeping across it, underneath the arches there remain these temples and shrines around Hyakkaen still carrying a little of the atmosphere of Edo.

Hyakkaen is located a few minutes from Tamanoi Station on the Tobu Line from Asakusa. It is closed on Mondays.

Nakano's Park for Thinkers

Tetsugakudo Park   哲学堂公園

Tetsugakudo in Nakano Ward is a park for thinkers. It was conceived as such by Enryo Inoue (1858-1919), the founder of Tetsugakukan University, later named Toyo University. Inoue had become concerned at the degree of Westernization taking place in Japan after the Meiji Restoration and set about countering it by encouraging Eastern thought. Tetsugakudo was opened in 1906 as part of Inoue's desire to promote the pursuit of enlightenment in general.

The main entrance consists of two stone posts. The one on the right is inscribed with the words "the gate of philosophy" *(tetsugakukan)* and the one on the left with the words "the world of truth" *(shinrikai)*.

To the left inside this gateway is the Philosophy Arch enclosing the ghost of an old woman to the left and a goblin to the right. The former is said to refer to the spiritual world and the latter to the materialistic world. This archway leads out onto the summit of the park, an area of level land on the top of Wada Hill.

Looking around the roof of the park in clockwise fashion from the archway, the small hill to the left is crowned by a triangular structure representing the three religions of Shintoism, Confucianism and Buddhism. Next to this is Universe Hall, so called because the truths of philosophy are contained in the secrets of the universe. Beside this building is a haunted plum tree.

The Castle of Absolutism is the name given to the library, reading being one key to philosophical understanding, while the next building, the Shiseido, is dedicated to the four great thinkers: Confucius, Buddha, Socrates and Kant. This building, which stands directly opposite the Philosophy Arch, was actually the first building to be placed in the park, in 1904.

Between Universe Hall and the library is the Bridge of Idealism, a stone bridge crossing a dry stream and leading down into the garden of the park. In terms of scenery, the view widens out and you are looking down among the trees and shrubbery.

In terms of philosophy, the visitor begins to lose his way, having left the summit of reason. Following the river you come to the small Spiritual Garden, with its Bridge of Conception and the Devil's Lamp. And nearby is the Apriori Spring, referring to the insights to be gained beyond the bounds of experience and education. It is now dried up and the visitor must search for the fountain of knowledge elsewhere.

At this point you are faced with a choice of how to return to the summit. Two paths lead up from the Spiritual Garden. You can choose the shortcut by taking the Route of Intuition, or you can tackle the longer Route of Understanding. Situated midway up the latter route is Deduction Point, an umbrella-shaped rest-place where the visitor is invited to stop and contemplate before proceeding further. Whichever path you choose, they come out at the same place, the Station of Consciousness. Here you can pause and, looking down the two routes, reflect on your decision.

Alternatively, you can follow the Myoshoji River along to that other scenic spot of philosophy, the Materialist Garden. On the way you pass the Tannuki Lamp. Man is possessed by both good and evil. The Tannuki Lamp represents the former, while the Devil's Lamp in the Spiritual Garden signifies the later.

There are numerous other objects dotted around the park, all designed to stimulate the philosophical mind. And if by the end of a thoughtful walk the various trails have left you a little bewildered, it is comforting to know that you can leave Tetsugakudo by the Common Sense Gate.

Tetsugakudo Park is reached from Araiyakushimae Station on the Seibu Shinjuku Line. The road leading across the railway line away to the north reaches Tetsugakudo in about 10 minutes.

88 Scenic Spots in One

Rikugien   六義園

Trees spill over the top of the mellow brick wall enclosing Rikugien, holding out the promise of plenty. Along a quiet outside street, it's not uncommon to find several parked cars, their drivers asleep in the calm that surrounds this exquisite garden.

Once inside, it is the turn of the outside world to impinge — less attractively — upon Rikugien, in the form of apartment buildings that have sprung up beyond the northeast wall. But look the other way and it is still possible to see uninterrupted a matured version of the garden first landscaped by the feudal lord Yoshiyasu Yanagisawa at the end of the 17th century.

Yanagisawa (1678-1714) entered the service of the Tokugawa government in 1690, the year that Tsunayoshi became the fifth shogun. A man of considerable literary attainments, Yanagisawa enjoyed the favor of the new shogun and in 1695 was granted an area of farmland outside Tokyo in Komagome Village. It was here that he constructed Rikugien, a labor of seven years.

The name Rikugien, reflecting Yanagisawa's love of learning, refers to the six principles behind the composition of classical Chinese poetry. In addition, 88 scenic spots — the sheer number is an indication of the garden's scope — were selected and named after celebrated places and sights in the literature and legends of China and Japan.

Although Rikugien went to seed for nearly a century after Yanagisawa's death in 1714, it was tidied up in 1810 and restored to its original beauty when it became part of the Iwasaki household in the early years of Meiji. In 1938 Baron Iwasaki presented the garden to the Tokyo metropolitan government, and that year it was opened to the public.

Like Korakuen, Rikugien is a stroll garden. Lake, artificial hill, waterfall, island, bridge, tea house and above all the exuberant trees blend to offer the visitor a constantly shifting panorama. There is a signposted route to follow, and many tempting diversions along the way.

Rikugien is closed on Mondays, or the day after if Monday coincides with a national holiday. Entrance costs ¥100. Within its walls, but separate from the garden, is a children's playground and sports area.

Rikugien

The entrance to Rikugien is a 10-minute walk from JNR Komagome Station on the Yamanote Line.

A Surprise at Every Corner

Arisugawa Memorial Park   有栖川宮記念公園

One of the pleasant things about visiting places is that they often turn up surprises, little extras which add to the enjoyment provided by the main purpose of the trip. A hidden shrine here, an interesting legend there. . . .

A visit to the Arisugawa Memorial Park in Tokyo's Azabu district provides just such a surprise. The park is laid out around a hill, at the foot of which is a pond ringed by amateur anglers, with streams and even a waterfall around it.

The park is well wooded, paths span out in all directions, and several bridges contribute to the scenery, including the Taikobashi (Drum Bridge). Eventually one of the paths leads you up to the flat area on top of the hill, wide enough for a good game of badminton.

And here's the little surprise, quite out of place, but equally charming — a statue of a newspaper delivery boy by Kyoko Asakura, dedicated to those youngsters who get up early each morning, whatever the weather, to make sure we get our news in time for breakfast. Newspaper delivery and the Arisugawa family, who once owned the land where the park now is, don't seem to have any clear connection, but it's a good chance to remember an important type of work.

As well as being hidden in the shade of some trees, the newspaper delivery boy is dwarfed by the nearby statue of Arisugawa Taruhito (1835-1895) on horseback. The Arisugawa family was founded in the 17th century as a branch of the imperial family, and took the name in 1672.

The lineage expired in 1913, after 288 years and 10 generations. One of the most famous members of the family was the said

Taruhito, an important figure in the Meiji Restoration. He commanded the army that put down the last remaining opposition in 1868-69, and also led troops in the suppression of the Satsuma rebellion of 1877. He died during the war against China.

The park is surrounded by embassies and temples. For a taste of the latter, where the road from the park returns to the station, turn left and walk to Tengenji-bashi Bridge. Then turn left into Meiji Dori, and the first temple on the left is Tengenji, said to have been built in 1717.

Keep walking, and just beyond the Esso station is Korinji Temple and another little surprise. In the graveyard here is buried Henry Heusken (1832-61), a Dutchman who studied Japanese in America and came to Japan as interpreter for Townsend Harris in 1856.

Heusken was killed by a group seeking the expulsion of foreigners, and a Japanese gravestone with a cross inscribed on it marks the place of his burial at Korinji.

A little further along the road is Myoshoji Temple, not open to the public, but apparently built by the Bakufu to act as protector of the Azabu Yakuen (herb garden) which was located in the district. Nearby is the Yakuenzaka, one of many narrow hills in the Minami Azabu area.

Follow one of these hills northward, away from Meiji Dori, and you eventually come to Sendaizaka and the more famous Zenpukuji Temple. If there's one thing that walking up and down the Azabu hills teaches you, it's that the job of the newspaper delivery boy can be no easy task.

Arisugawa Memorial Park is located a short distance from Hiro-O Station on the Hibiya subway line.

Yokohama's Back Garden

Sankeien 三溪園

Although bearing no traces of the commercial boom which hit Yokohama after the opening of the port in 1859, Sankeien Garden is as much a testimony to that period as the architecture of the city itself. For the garden, nestled into the coastal area to the south of the city, was built by Tomitaro Hara (1868-1939), one of the Meiji generation of businessmen who made his fortune as an exporter of raw silk.

The relationship between art and wealth is an ambiguous one, but like many other millionaires, Hara turned his money over to the propagation of art. One result was the splendid Sankeien Garden, the private residence of the Hara family which was opened to the public as early as 1906.

The grounds are made up of an inner garden, opened in 1958, and the sprawling outer garden and the whole atmosphere is typically Japanese with the sense of relaxed balance between the natural and the imposed. The name Sankeien, which Hara took as his pseudonym, is taken from the fact that there are three low hills in the park and the gardens are landscaped around them.

Situated inside the grounds are several buildings of great cultural importance, each a museum unto itself without detracting from the pine hills and the silent ponds around them. A wooden boat sitting in the pond near the main entrance adds a touch of domesticity to the picture.

Rising over the park without dominating it is the three-story pagoda, perched on a hill and suitably requiring the visitor to ascend a steep slope to meet it. The pagoda, 25 meters high, was brought to Sankeien in 1914 from Tomyoji Temple in Kyoto. Its red color contrasting with the surrounding foliage, the pagoda is said to be a good example of Muromachi architecture and the oldest of its kind in the Kanto area.

The most stately building in the park is the Rinshun-kaku, located in the inner garden and consisting of three buildings facing a quiet pond, typical of the villas built by feudal lords in the Tokugawa Period. The Rinshun-kaku, which was brought to Sankeien in 1915, was originally built in 1649 and was located within the Iwade Palace in Wakayama Prefecture. The low, light structures possess a delicacy which is reflected on the decorated screens and sliding doors.

Other buildings in the park include a kind of mausoleum, brought from Kyoto in 1902; the Gekka-den, a guest house for feudal lords which was brought to Sankeien in 1918; the two-story Choshu-kaku house, presented to Hara in 1922; a fragile-looking tea arbor and an old convent once used by women as a refuge place from their fearful husbands. The latter was brought to Sankeien from Tokeiji Temple in Kamakura.

A more recent addition to the park is the farmhouse of the Yanohara family which used to be situated in Gifu Prefecture but, threatened with destruction as a result of the construction of the Mihoro Dam, was donated to the Sankeien Garden by its owner in 1960. Originally built over 200 years ago, the farmhouse has the architectural style characteristic of upper class rural dwellings of the time.

Take bus No. 54 from Negishi Station on the Keihin Tohoku Line. Entrance to Sankeien is from the Honmoku Civil Park bus stop.

Sunshine and Bikes Spell Fun

Cycling Parks　　　　　　　　　泉自然公園／森林公園

A trip out into the countryside, a bit of healthy exercise, a stroll among the trees and flowers, and then a restful picnic spread out on the grass. What more could you ask of a day's outing?

These attractions are offered by cycling parks, two of the best of which are located a comfortable one or two hours from inside Tokyo, on opposite sides of the capital.

Izumi Shizen Koen was opened in 1969 in Chiba. The cycling course, a bargain at ¥200 for three hours, takes you from the entrance of the park round its circumference, past a splendid lotus pond and out into the open fields with their plots of potatoes, peanuts, rice and corn.

The turning point for the course, which in total covers 13 km, is another park, Heiwa Koen. From there the route back takes you along the road round the other side of Izumi Park until you reach the entrance again.

Then comes the restful part. Izumi Park is divided into a number of separate areas, such as the bird forest, apple and plum gardens, maple and cedar forests, Ohanami Hiroba for cherry blossoms, and an iris garden. A long narrow lake stretches around one side of the park, crossed by the 60-m long Izumi Suspension Bridge.

After the energy-consuming bicycle course, it's a wonderful feeling to stretch out on the gentle-sloping grass areas and watch the clear sky through the towering trees, serenaded by an unrelenting cicada chorus.

Izumi Shizen Koen is located 20 minutes from Keisei Chiba Station by Keisei bus bound for Naruto, leaving from bus stands Nos. 4 and 5. The Izumi Shizen Koen Iriguchi bus stop is on

National Highway 126, and the park entrance is a signposted 10-minute walk away.

The second cycling park worth a visit is **Musashi Kyuryo Shinrin Koen** in Saitama. Planned to commemorate the 100th anniversary of Meiji and aimed at preserving the Musashino environment, the park was opened in 1972. Set in 3 sq. km of red pines, oaks and grass areas, with 41 marshes dotted around here and there, the park provides a varied cycling course.

In the southern part of the park there is a flower garden and playground and sports areas; in the central part there is a central square, sculpture square, a stream square and a museum; and the western part has similar spots, including a "mischief square" for younger visitors.

Shinrin Park, closed on Mondays, is located just over an hour from Ikebukuro on the Tobu Tojo Line, getting off at Shinrin Koen Station. The cycling center, with tandems available, is situated by the central entrance. Both Izumi Park and Shinrin Park — fortunately — have fewer commercial facilities available than usual, so it's advisable to take along a picnic box.

Row, Row, Row Your Boat . . .

Boating Lakes　　　　　　千鳥ケ淵公園／井の頭公園ほか

"Indoor game centers are bad for business," sighs a ruddy Tokyo boatkeeper who has seen her custom fall away in recent years. But despite this lady's lament, there are still plenty of places left in Tokyo to hire rowboats.

In central Tokyo the pastime should be called "moating." Right by the New Otani Hotel is the **Akasakamitsuke Boto-jo,** which utilizes part of the former outer moat surrounding the Imperial Palace. To one side towers the 40-story New Otani, held back by a cordon of trees, to the other an elevated expressway curves round as if to keep the moat in check.

Less intimidating is **Chidorigafuchi,** by the Budokan, the other stretch of imperial moat (in this case inner moat) open to the public. Though the walled sides are imposing, they aren't as menacing as an expressway. Nearest stations are Takeshiba or Kudanshita on the Tozai Line. The boathouse is right opposite the Fairmont Hotel.

Also popular is **Shinobazu Pond** in Ueno. The boating pond is part of a larger stretch of water covered in a spectacular blanket of lotus flowers. In the distance, the pagoda near Toshogu Shrine rises mysteriously. Ueno Station is a short walk away.

The **Tama River** offers the most scope for lusty oarsmen. In theory it should be possible to row as far as Haneda, but take a spare pair of shoes if planning to catch a plane as the boathouse looks after the pair you arrive in. A short walk from Tamagawaen Station on the Toyoko Line, boating from Maruko Bridge makes up in sheer scope what it lacks in appealing scenery.

On an altogether different scale is **Himonya Park,** just down the Toyoko Line near Gakugeidaigaku Station. The park has a small duck pond that can be circled in a few minutes, a shrine on a tiny island reached by humpbacked bridge, and goats and ponies in a small children's zoo.

Said to be the place where the Buddhist priest Nichiren bathed his feet many centuries ago, **Senzoku Pond** is similarly a quiet, local park. Situated right by Senzokuike Station on the Ikegami Line, the pond is of modest proportions and surrounded by a narrow band of greenery. There is an island at one end.

In the western suburbs of Tokyo, three large and wooded parks cast in the same mold have good boating facilities. **Inokashira Park,** a 10-minute walk from the Chuo Line's Kichijoji Station or alternatively reached on the Inokashira Line (alight at Inokashira Koen Station), is in the spring a spectacular setting for boating as the lake is ringed by cherry trees.

Zenpukuji Park, to the north of the Chuo Line and a short bus ride away from Kichijoji, Nishi Ogikubo or Ogikubo stations, is in a quiet residential area. Divided in two by a road, one half of the park contains a pond, the other a boating lake.

Located not far from the Seibu Ikebukuro Line station of the same name, **Shakuji Park,** 4 km north of Zenpukuji, in Nerima Ward, is also split by a road. To one side lies a long boating lake, to the other, the rounder, pine-encircled Samboji Pond.

Shakuji Park is popular with anglers, as is another smaller boating park in the area, **Musashiseki Park,** just inside the western extremes of Suginami Ward. Boats are for hire on an oblong-shaped lake. The park is actually nearer Higashi Fukumi Station than Musashiseki Station, both on the Seibu Shinjuku Line.

In most cases, boating is not available from December to March. Prices range from the inexpensive — ¥100 per 30 minutes at Himonya and Musashiseki parks — to the reasonable — ¥350 per hour at Ueno — to the dear — ¥700 per hour at Akasakamitsuke, in the vicinity of three or four major hotels. There's a moral here somewhere.

Looking Out to Sea

Kannonzaki Park 観音崎公園

There is always something mysterious about a lighthouse. Usually standing isolated, a single tower rooted on land yet calling out to sea. The solitary keeper guiding ships in their lonely fight against the waves. It is the lighthouse that somehow best highlights the romance and adventure of the sea.

Kannonzaki lighthouse looks out over the Uraga Strait, the strip of water at the entrance to Tokyo Bay and the scene of a busy shipping line occupied by yachts and tankers alike. The sparkling white lighthouse, on the southeastern tip of Miura Peninsula, commands a magnificent view of the seascape which spreads out in front of it.

A Frenchman, Francois Leon Verny, was the designer of the lighthouse which began operating on Jan. 1, 1869. Verny originally arrived in Japan in 1865 to take charge of the Yokosuka iron foundry, but he then took on the task of constructing Japan's first western-style lighthouse in Kannonzaki. This he followed by designing other lighthouses, including the Shinagawa lighthouse in 1870, before returning to concentrate on the iron foundry.

The original lighthouse, built of stone, was damaged in an earthquake in 1922 and the second structure suffered the same fate at the hands of the Kanto Earthquake of 1923. The present structure, the third, was put up in 1925. Made of concrete, it stands 15 meters off the ground and 56 meters above sea level.

It is possible to climb the narrow, twisting stairs of the lighthouse and enjoy the view of the busy shipping channel. The light from the lighthouse reaches 37 km out to sea and flashes at 13-second intervals.

At nighttime, there is therefore a wonderful view of the flashing beacon and the lights of ships passing through the strait. In the daytime, the hills of Boso Peninsula on the other side of the channel present an attractive view on a clear day.

The view becomes even more striking if one leaves the lighthouse and climbs the wooded hills. The white, octagonal lighthouse, set against blue sky and thick green forestry, presents a most picturesque sight. The setting is Kannonzaki Park (the name, by the way, being taken from a temple which used to be situated in the area) which offers a pleasant background of quiet avenues for casual hiking. These hills are a haven of bird and insect noises and various kinds of trees and plants.

The path leading away from the lighthouse through the park takes you to observation point 1, close to which is located a monument dedicated to those seamen who lost their lives during the Pacific War.

Beyond this monument, past the fountain square toward the hotel, you will find a bus stop. From here a bus takes you back to Uraga, completing a round trip to Kannonzaki Park. Uraga itself, now a commercial dockyard port, flourished during the Edo Period as a strategic point at the entrance to Edo. It was the port where all vessels were inspected before entering the bay. And it was also the spot where in 1853 Commodore Perry's squadron dropped anchor with the famous letter seeking the opening of Japanese ports to American commerce.

The walk from the lighthouse is well-guided by maps and signposts and taken casually, as it should be, requires from two to three hours to complete.

Take the Keihin Kyuko express train from Shinagawa, changing onto the local line at Horinouchi for Uraga. The journey takes about one hour, and the bus from Uraga to Kannonzaki about 15 minutes.

Good for Plane Spotting, too

Oi Bird Park 　　　　　　　　　　　　　　　大井野鳥公園

"It's a good place for plane spotting, too," concedes a member of Japan's Wild Bird Association of the wild bird park at Oi. Situated close to Haneda Airport — so close it seems almost possible to reach out and touch the jets as they take off and land —the park manages to sustain a flourishing and cosmopolitan community of birds quite unperturbed by the comings and goings of the jets.

Oi Wild Bird Park was opened by the Tokyo metropolitan government in April 1978 on land reclaimed from Tokyo Bay in the 1960s. The seventh park to have been opened under the "Maritime Park Plan," the wild bird park is one of a number of projects stimulated by community action to preserve nature in the area.

The results are looking good, for although the park shares the sprawl of land refill with major roads, factories and warehouses, it is said that in the course of a year it plays host to about half the 500 species of bird seen in Japan. These include ducks, gulls, swallows, coots, snipes and migratory herons, the latter using the park as a temporary resting place on their journey from Siberia to the southern hemisphere.

The bird park itself, which includes Ban Pond, is quite small and not accessible to the public. Visitors view the interior from an observation platform at one corner. A diagram explains where to look for the birds — on distant telephone lines, at water's edge, in bushes, trees, and on the pond itself.

Contiguous with the park is a larger area of grassy land, also around a pond, which is open to the public all the time. Wild birds have been gathering in their numbers around these two ponds, Ban and Shioiri, since the early 1970s and it's thanks to this other pond that the bird park thrives so.

Unless one possesses binoculars and a telescope and knows what to look for, bird watching can be a little frustrating. Therefore it is useful to know that on the first Sunday of every month a few dozen members of the Tokyo branch of the Japan Wild Bird Association gather at Oi Bird Park for a three-hour ramble around neighboring Shioiri Pond.

You don't have to be a member to participate, but everyone is charged ¥200. For this you will find yourself in the company of knowledgeable ornithologists with binoculars and telescopes galore.

Bird parks are few and far between in Japan. There is only one bird sanctuary, at Utonaiko in Hokkaido, which coincidentally is also located near an airport, Sapporo's Chitose. Therefore it is a credit to congested Tokyo that it has found room for birds as well as men.

Following rain, the area around Shioiri Pond is quite marshy and it is advisable to wear boots. Also recommended is a packed lunch, as there are no shops or restaurants nearby.

For those who would like further information about Japan's birds, the Japan Wild Bird Association is located in the Aoyama Flower Building, 1-4 Shibuya 1-chome, Shibuya Ward, Tokyo 150, tel. (03) 406-7141.

Take a bus from Oimachi Station bound for Shinagawa Station, or vice versa, and alight at Oi Dai-Nana Koen-shita. There is also a bus from Omori Station. Alternatively, take the monorail from Hamamatsucho Station and alight at Ritsu-Senta-mae. The park is a 15-minute walk from there.

Museum Parks

Ome Railway Park

A Haven for Naturalists

Roka Park

蘆花恒春園

There are many places in and around Tokyo maintained to commemorate leading figures of the past, but surely none as well preserved and unspoiled as Roka Koshunen Garden in Setagaya Ward.

This was the site where the novelist Kenjiro Tokutomi (pen name Roka) spent the second half of his life. Tokutomi is famous for having written such novels as "The Cuckoo" and "Gibberish of an Earthworm." He died in 1927 at the age of 60, midway through four volumes of confessions which his wife Aiko duly completed for him.

It was Aiko who spearheaded the movement to preserve Tokutomi's belongings, donating the site to Tokyo in 1937. The authorities then decided that as the former dwellings of Shakespeare and Goethe were preserved in their respective countries, so Japan similarly should follow suit and honor its literary greats. The park was opened in 1938.

Once through the main gate, it is indeed like entering someone's back garden. No effort has been made to clear up the withered tree trunks and cobwebs, and the result is very appealing. Tokutomi, a great naturalist, would have been delighted.

The novelist moved to this site, where he lived a secluded and rural life style, after a trip to Jerusalem and a visit to Tolstoy in Russia. The residence and study quarters have been preserved as they were, together with books, manuscripts and articles of daily use which belonged to Tokutomi. In the display kept in a separate exhibition room can be found, among other things, a letter to the Meiji novelist from Tolstoy and a collection of Tolstoy's works.

24

The park is open from 9 a.m. to 4:30 p.m. and closed on Mondays. The display room is open only on Sundays and national holidays, and then only from 1 to 4 p.m.

The feeling of seclusion which Tokutomi seems to have strived for is maintained among the beech and Japanese oak trees and general ground foliage. There is also a bamboo copse which Tokutomi is said to have planted himself, and in a far corner of the garden can be found the couple's graves. Retaining the quality of nature found in western Tokyo in the past, Roka Park certainly provides for a quiet, contemplative visit.

Roka Park

Roka Park is reached by taking the Keio Line from Shinjuku, getting off at Roka Koen Station, from where it is a 15-minute walk to the south.

It'll Never Happen to Me . . .

Earthquake Memorial Museum   東京慰霊堂

"Conflagration subsequent to severe earthquake at Yokohama at noon today. Whole city practically ablaze with numerous casualties. All traffic stopped."

That was the first message to be sent out to the world following the Great Kanto Earthquake, which struck Tokyo and the surrounding regions on the morning of Sept. 1, 1923. It was transmitted from a ship in Tokyo Bay at 8 p.m. that same evening, at which time the extent of the disaster was still not known. For it was not only Yokohama, but the whole Kanto area that had been hit.

The earthquake occurred at 11:58 a.m. just as people were beginning to prepare their lunches. This meant that explosion after explosion took place, leading to fires which whipped through the wooden structures of the city. And as the fires raged, tremors also continued into the next day. People grabbed whatever belongings they could and raced for cover in whatever refuge places they could find.

One of those refuges was at Yokoami, near Ryogoku in Sumida Ward. A small area previously used by the Ministry of War as a clothing depot, the spot was bought by the Tokyo government in July 1923, a couple of months before the earthquake struck. People took refuge there, but the fire spread around the area, engulfing the people. It is said that as many as 28,000 perished there, and from being a refuge center, the spot came to be used as a mass funeral ground.

The park is dominated by the huge memorial hall, topped by a three-story pagoda, with the charnel house below. This extremely modest, yet imposing stucture is said to contain the remains of some 58,000 people, victims of the great earthquake, and later of the World War II bombings. In a corner to one side of the memorial hall is a bell tower, presented by Chinese Buddhists in memory of the victims of the earthquake in October 1925.

The park now serves as an excellent play area for children, playing hide-and-seek among the various other memorial stones, while in another corner is the Memorial Museum, housing an exhibition on the Great Kanto Earthquake and earthquakes in general. Outside the entrance can be seen the burnt-out remains of a car and other machinery destroyed in the earthquake.

Inside the museum, on the first floor, are numerous exhibits telling the tale of destruction. Melted buttons and beer bottles from Chiyoda Ward; melted sugar from Koto Ward; charcoaled biscuits from a cake shop in Shinbashi; a Japanese-language dictionary, the only one remaining out of 500 stocked together on the second floor of a building in Chiyoda Ward; and a burnt fragment of a Noh song script, said to have been blown 58 km into Chiba Prefecture, where it was found, by the fiery wind. There is also a tree with part of a roof wrapped around it, next to a photograph of the spot where it was found.

The final sections of the museum are devoted to the World War II bombings, and to information on what to do in the event of an earthquake. The museum is open from 9 a.m. to 4:30 p.m., closed on Mondays, and admission is free. It is well worth a visit, not only for its recording of the earthquake disaster, but also as a valuable social history museum.

Earthquake Memorial Museum park is located a 10-minute walk from Ryogoku Station on the JNR Sobu Line.

Old Rural Houses Preserved

Nihon Minkaen 日本民家園

Japanese housing is a complex issue. Respected abroad for the beauty of its style, resented at home for its lack of spaciousness; lauded for its functionalism, yet bemoaned for its effect on the individual's private life. The Japanese house is without doubt unique and that distinct style — the simplicity of design, the flexibility of the wooden structure, the prevalence of natural colors — is so deeply rooted that it continues today even where western appearances are taking over.

In 1965, the city of Kawasaki began the task of preserving some of the best examples of Japanese housing styles of the past. The result is 17 structures, including a shrine and a Kabuki stage, taken from various localities around the country and relocated in the wooded hills of Ikuta Park in Kawasaki. The historical dwellings are shown as they were originally lived in two to three centuries ago, with various utensils, tools and furniture also displayed. The visitor is free to wander in and out of the houses and, given that this is an outdoor museum, breathe in the atmosphere of Japan's past.

The first surprising thing is the size of the homes, being much larger than the structures now seen crowded into Tokyo's limited space. The fact is that these houses have been brought from the countryside where families were larger and where the work of the family was closely connected with the home. Thus, for example, the house of the Suzuki family was also used as an inn for horse traders, the horses having been kept in the dirt-floor part of the house while the dealers, on their way to auction, would stay on the second floor or, if they were more wealthy, maybe in the guest rooms at the back.

28

It must also be remembered that these houses were the dwellings of relatively rich sections of rural society. The dwellings of Ito and Sasaki were those of village heads and that of the Misawa family was the home of an assistant to the village head. As such, life appears to have been more comfortable than it must have been for those lower classes of society not represented here.

The influence of locality and climate is clearly seen in the structures. The Misawa family house, built 130 years ago, was located in the windy region of Ina City, in Nagano Prefecture, so that the design is typically stout and sound with a shingle roof weighted down with rocks. The house was built low to reduce the damaging effect of the winds. The former dwelling of the Sasaki family, on the other hand, was located in Minami Saku in Nagano, an area of light snowfall such that the stoutness gives way to a much lighter structure consisting of relatively thin pillars and beams.

One of the most fascinating of the houses displayed is the former dwelling of the Yamashita family from Shirakawa village in Gifu Prefecture, built some 150 years ago with a steep rafter design enabling it to withstand heavy snowfall. The second floor of this four-story building is presented as an exhibition room, showing various folkcraft goods and wares, ranging from the intriguing hanging pots, old furniture and tableware to rifles and armor.

The interest of this house lies not only in its design, but also in the sociology of the family which occupied it. Shirakawa was a village which due to the surrounding high mountains lived in isolation until into the Meiji Period. It lived its own life based on agriculture and sericulture. As a result, a large family system developed to support the home's economy and to prevent the home from splitting up. As many as 30 to 40 family members could be living in a house similar to the Yamashitas', and to protect the family group, only the eldest son was able to marry formally. This was a distinct form of the family found only in the northwestern part of Gifu.

Ikuta Park is also the site of the Youth Science Museum, opened in 1971 by the city of Kawasaki as a science center to help spread knowledge of the sciences, and of astronomy in particular. It is designed especially for young people and is often used for school research trips. The focal point of the center is the dome of the planetarium, where visitors can view the constellations. The program of the planetarium changes each month.

Entrance to the park is free, but entrance to the houses costs ¥300 and the planetarium ¥20. The museum park, like the planetarium, is closed on Mondays.

Nihon Minkaen

Take the express train to Mukogaokayuen Station on the Odakyu Line, about 20 minutes from Shinjuku. From the south exit, walk along by the side of the monorail to Fuchu Kendo main road. Cross this road, and the park is about 500 meters along the small road leading away from you.

Reconstructing Setagaya's Past

Okamoto Minkaen   岡本民家園

Okamoto Minkaen was opened in December 1980, its aim being to preserve a little of Setagaya Ward's past and to offer a glimpse of what life must have been like in the area in the middle years of the Edo Period.

The main thatched house was previously lived in by Magoyoshi Nagasaki of Setagaya Ward, and was presented by him to the ward as a cultural asset in April 1977. There then followed an investigation of the house's history and a collection of the items in it, after which it was decided to set it up in Okamoto Park.

Stooping through the front door entrance, the first thing that hits you is the darkness. And then the smoke, which billows from a large stove on the earthen floor, apparently to keep insects away from the fine timber beams.

Climbing up from the earthen floor, the house consists of four basic rooms: a drawing room *(zashiki)*, a guest room *(dei)* with its *tokonoma* alcove, a back room *(nando)*, and what might be called the living room *(chanoma)*. In the latter there is a hanging pot over a hearth, from which visitors are welcome to draw water and make a pot of tea.

Okamoto Minkaen is of course on a smaller scale than the Nihon Minkaen, but it does have this advantage of offering a personal approach. Visitors are warmly welcomed at the reception room which houses a collection of photos concerning the house and items belonging to it, traces of the past such as old papers, books and so on.

Moreover, the policy has been not simply to preserve the house, but also to reconstruct the farming environment around it. In front

31

of the house, therefore, is a small vegetable patch, and behind it are bamboo trees.

There is also a storehouse, again donated by a resident of Setagaya. This storehouse, built in the middle of the 19th century, was apparently unique in having a stone roof, and particularly noticeable are the curving beams of the structure. It is now used for showing films about Okamoto Minkaen, and about old houses in general.

The Nagasaki house actually passed through 11 generations up to its retirement, reflecting indeed the strength of timber structures. Toward the end of the 17th century, a family of four, headed by one Nagasaki Magobei, left the main Nagasaki household, consisting of some 40 members, to set up their own home in Setagaya.

After about 100 years and much hard work by the family, the fourth Magobei was able to rebuild the house. As it was a time of severe shortages and impoverishment, however, it was impossible for him to build a really large house. The house that was built then is the one on display now.

The Nagasaki household continued to prosper — the sixth Magobei being chosen as village representative and the house being renovated with main pillars, a sign of the family's status, being used. Part of the family's prosperity was the result of silk-raising being added to their agricultural work.

Okamoto Minkaen is located at 19-1, Okamoto 2-chome, tel. 03-709-6959. Admission is free. It is open from 9:30 a.m. to 4:30 p.m., and closed on Mondays and national holidays.

Take the bus for Seijogakuenmae Station from Futakotamagawa-en Station on the Shin-Tamagawa Line. Get off at the stop for Kinuta Kogyo High School, cross the Tamazutsumi main road and head north down past the school. A 5-minute walk brings you to the museum house.

A Park for All Seasons

Koganei Park 小金井公園

Whether it's romping over open spaces with the kids or gazing at the changing colors of the trees; kicking your way through piles of fallen leaves or hunting for acorns; flying kites at New Year's or enjoying cherry blossom viewing, Koganei Park seems to offer the opportunity for just about everything.

Located some 20 km to the west of Tokyo, Koganei Park is wide enough in area to absorb groups of schoolchildren and picnickers, and cozy enough for the more romantic or the solitary. There is a cycling center with courses provided, an archery range and plenty of open space for Frisbee and badminton adventurists.

In the spirit of all-round development, moreover, a large corner of the park is devoted to the Musashino Kyodokan (Musashino Provincial Museum). The stylish building which now houses this museum was removed and reconstructed at the present site in 1941 from the plaza in front of the Imperial Palace and was used as a training center during the war.

The Musashino region has been a very rich area in terms of archaeological discoveries and the museum displays some 1,300 of them, from straw-rope patterned earthenware of the Jomon Period (Japan's Neolithic Period up to about 200 B.C.) to more recent agricultural implements. The items are set out in simple chronological order for clarity and there is an introduction in English explaining briefly how life must have been when the sea actually reached as far as the Musashino area, the rise of settlements, society based on rice cultivation and the emergence of classes.

After this short introduction, the English explanations unfortunately disappear, but the displayed items in themselves give a little taste of the changes of history. Most were excavated from the Koganei, Kokubunji, Chofu and Sayama areas. There are wooden irrigation pipes as used on the Tamagawa River and folkcraft items such as lamps and candlestands.

The items displayed within the museum walls take on an added interest when seen together with the outdoor display, the pride of the park. There always seems to be something more refreshing about an outdoor museum, and Koganei Park has a fine Kodai Mura, a village of ancient dwellings, and an Edo Village.

The ancient village consists of dugout dwellings of the Jomon Period and the Yayoi Period (from 200 B.C. until about 200 A.D.) and a raised floor warehouse, together with ancient burial mounds, tombs belonging to the highest class at the earliest stage of Japanese history.

As for the Edo Village, there is the headman's house, brought to this spot from what is now Nozaki in Mitaka, where it had been the house of the Yoshino family; a very imposing gate of a *daimyo* lord's house built in the Taisho Period, brought from Minato Ward in Tokyo; a locksmith's house, and a hall of votive wooden tablets on which are painted horses. These tablets, called *ema,* are traditionally offered at shrines in prayer for good luck.

Koganei Park itself was opened to the public in January 1954, after having been established in 1940 in commemoration of the 2,600th anniversary of the imperial reign. It is open from 9 a.m. until 5 p.m. and closed on Mondays.

Koganei Park is located a 10-minute walk from Hana-Koganei Station on the Seibu Shinjuku Line, or a short bus ride from Musashi-Koganei Station on the Chuo Line.

Excavations in the Tama Hills

Machida Iseki Park   町田遺跡公園

Japanese history is not all stories about temples and shrines and samurai. Archaeological discoveries since World War II have been gradually pushing back the time span during which these islands have been occupied by man and several important excavations have revealed traces of social life which help to make Japan's prehistory clearer.

The Tama hills to the south of Tokyo have proved to be a rich source of material. Lying in the southern part of those hills, the city of Machida has now earned a reputation as a typical modern bed-town serving the Tokyo metropolis. In the 1960s it was realized that many valuable remains lay under the soils of Machida and plans to raise large housing complexes in the area threatened to bury them forever.

Machida, with the help of Rissho University, therefore carried out a survey of the area, beginning in 1968. Several historic sites and remains were unearthed and one spot in particular revealed traces of former dwellings several thousand years old. That site has now been preserved as a park, suitably named Iseki (meaning "ruins") Park, located in Honmachida, the central part of Machida itself.

Altogether traces of 11 former dwellings were discovered, four from the prehistoric Jomon Period and seven from the later Yayoi Period, and two of these, one from each period, have been restored to their original appearance.

Life during the Jomon Period, which is dated from some 10,000 years ago, was basically a hunting one. The people lived by hunting the birds and animals, especially deer and bear, which occupied the hills, as well as by eating the surrounding vegetation. Earthenware and stoneware of the period have been discovered and some simple tools unearthed. It appears that the people lived in small villages of 10 or so dwellings built in clusters together.

The Yayoi Period, dating from some 2,000 years ago, followed the Jomon Period and was marked by profound changes in the life of the people in the sense that agriculture began to take over from hunting. In particular, rice became predominant, leading to a more stable community life on a larger scale than before. Wooden farm implements appeared, together with stone tools and various bronze objects.

The structure near the entrance to Iseki Park is a dwelling of the Yayoi Period, with an area of some 30 square meters, while the Jomon dwelling occupies some 35 square meters. The construction of the thatched dwellings appears to have been similar, involving digging a hole in the ground, laying a floor, and then building the one-room structure around a frame of four vertical poles. Dwellings of the Jomon Period were basically circular, while Yayoi dwellings were increasingly square in appearance.

Starting point for a visit should be the Honmachida City Museum, where some 750 excavated objects from the area are on display, together with other folkcraft and artistic articles. In the entrance to the building is an excellent model of the topography of the Tama hills, showing Machida and the places where archaeological findings have been made.

The park is a three-minute walk up the hill from the museum. The surrounding area is now firmly rooted in the modern *"danchi"* period, but a 15-minute walk down from Iseki Park leads to Yakushiike Park, the home of Yakushiike Temple, also known as Fukuoji Temple. The pond in the valley was built some 400 years ago for irrigation purposes and now, crossed by a bridge, acts as a calm focal point for the park.

Iseki Park can be reached by taking the bus for Fujinodai Danchi from Machida Station on the Odakyu Line, the required stop being at the Honmachida City Museum.

Heaps of Historical Garbage

Kasori Shell Mound 　　　　　　　　　加曾利貝塚

It seems there is more to garbage heaps than meets the eye, especially when the garbage in question consists of shells. Before realizing that shells could be put to use as tools or as decorative ornaments, the inhabitants of Japan in the Jomon Period apparently discarded them into what are now called shell mounds.

There are well over 1,000 places in Japan where Jomon Period shell mounds have been found, most of them left on the tops of hills a few kilometers from the coast, and most of them on the Pacific side of the country. Apparently people in the past thought this very strange, and assumed that some kind of giants must have eaten the shellfish from the sea and thrown the shells away on the tops of the hills.

Knowledge has since become more scientific, however and it is now known that, far from being mere dumping grounds, the shell mounds actually marked sites where old settlements used to be. The largest such shell mound so far unearthed in Japan is located in Chiba, near Makuhari and Inage, which are still today considered good places for collecting seashells.

The Kasori Shell Mound consists of two mounds, a north one and a south one together forming an unusual figure-8 shape. The northern mound has a diameter of 130 meters, and the south one a diameter of 170 meters, and excavations have yielded abundant evidence that settlements existed on the site.

Much earthenware has been found, as well as traces of dwellings, many stone, bone and shell implements, and some 60 skeletons. Analyses of the objects excavated have been able to date the Kasori *kaizuka* (shell mounds) to the Jomon Period.

Rising to 20-32 meters above sea level, the mounds were not simply places where waste shells were thrown away. It has been suggested that they represent places where shellfish were stripped and the contents dried and put into storage as an important food resource, perhaps also exchanged for stone materials to make arrowheads and so on, which would have been scarce in this area.

The northern part of the site has been turned into a park with a museum which opened to the public in November 1966. Just inside the entrance there is a map of the park. A path leads off to the left around the mound, and the first building contains a sectional cutting of part of a shell mound, showing the various layers of shells.

Follow the path round and you come to the museum, outside which is a reconstructed dugout dwelling of the mid-Jomon Period some 5,000 years ago. With a diameter of 5-6 meters and built around six pillars, such a dwelling would house four or five people.

The museum contains exhibits excavated on the site and descriptions of the kind of life which people living around Tokyo Bay in the Jomon Period must have led. There are also maps showing changes in the coastline and the distribution of shell mounds around the country, and various displays on shells and shell mound culture. Admission to the museum is ¥40 for adults and ¥20 for children under senior high school age.

The Kasori Shell Mound is situated about 30 minutes by bus from JNR Chiba Station. Take the bus from bus stop No. 6 bound for Chishirodai Shako, getting off at the Sakuragicho bus stop. The park is located nearby.

Railway Park in Ome Hills

Ome Railway Park   青梅鉄道公園

Despite constant fare increases and rush-hour congestion, JNR won over a few hearts recently on a trip to Osaka by the Shinkansen. Passing by towering Mt. Fuji on a clear day, the bullet train slowed down and all passengers were invited to enjoy the sight because, it was explained, "Fuji-san appears even more beautiful than ever today." "We'll make up the time afterward," the announcement concluded efficiently.

So with all grievances buried, it seems only right to pursue the new-found friendship further and visit the Railway Park in Ome, to the northwest of Tokyo. This park was opened in October 1962 by JNR to mark the 90th anniversary of the opening of the railroad in Japan. That first small step of 29.1 km has grown into an extensive JNR network of some 22,000 km, the frontier stretching from the northernmost station of Wakkanai to Yamagawa in the far south.

The charts on the walls of the exhibition hall tell the story. Those first trains jogged along at a leisurely 28.9 kph while the Shinkansen has itself leisurely passed the 250 kph-mark in test runs. The skip down to Osaka is done at a steady 180 kph.

The first floor of the hall is dominated in the middle by a large model train set, the "Railroad Panorama," which includes all the familiar local lines passing through miniature tunnels. With sounds included, it is sure to set the hearts of children and adults alike tingling. The surrounding walls are lined with models of trains and charts about the history of the railroad and the techniques of construction and operation.

There are several fascinating tidbits of information to be picked up. Commodore Perry brought the first model train set ever to be seen in Japan; the longest platform can be found at Kyoto Station, where Platform No. 1 extends 564 meters; the longest station name is that of Utsunomiya Kamotsu Terminal. Do you know which station has the shortest name?

The second floor of the hall consists of another model train set, with the Shinkansen vying with an older locomotive, while the surrounding walls carry a number of interesting photographs, charts and exhibits, such as rail tickets from the Meiji Period. Some of the information may be aging a little, but the whole thing is brought well up-to-date on the back wall of the first floor of the hall, where there is a running model of the next step forward, the linear motor car

Billed as the "railway of the future," this model zips along suspended in a magnetic field, holding out the promise of cutting the time of the trip from Tokyo to Osaka down to one hour in the future. That should cut Fuji-san down to size a bit as well. The linear motor car may be the answer to many pollution problems but it certainly leaves a chilling feeling as it speeds noiselessly along.

It's a relief to get back to the age of steam and memories of black engines belching smoke. Several locomotives are displayed outside like monuments to the period with the added attraction that you can climb up to the controls and get a firsthand touch of the age yourself.

Among them are a 110 type locomotive, build in Yorkshire, England, in 1871, which ran on the original line from Shinbashi to Yokohama and which weighs in at 22.3 tons; the 5500 type, a 30-ton tender built by Pier Peacock Co., also of England, and the majestic D51452, a handsome 78-tonner nicknamed "Degoichi." From 1936-46, 1,515 engines of this D51 type were built.

The outside display also includes a first-class passenger car, a dining car and a minitrain for children to ride on. Admission to the Railway Park is free and it is open from 9 a.m. to 4 p.m. It is closed on Mondays.

JNR must be congratulated, not only for providing an interesting museum, but also for placing it in the fine setting of the Ome hills.

These long, narrow hills extend from east to west to the north of Ome and are ideal for casual hiking. There are many well-trodden paths and many maps to point you in the right direction through the cedar trees.

One path leads out of the Railway Park and along the ridge past four rest places, from where you either hike right out into the hills or cut back down past Miyanotaira Station to the Tama River. A walk along the riverside back toward Ome brings you to Mizuno Park, the home of the Ome Municipal Museum of Provincial History. As the pamphlet says. "This museum was completed in 1973 by the collective will of the citizens who love both beautiful nature and traditional culture."

Admission to the museum is free and it is closed on Mondays. Walk back through the park and across the river and Ome Station is 10 minutes' walk away.

The Railway Park is reached by the Ome Line from Tachikawa Station (on the JNR Chuo Line), and is a well-signposted 15-minute walk from Ome Station up into the hills.

Admiral Togo's Flagship

Mikasa Park   三笠公園

There are said to be four great historical warships left in the world, preserved as museums and monuments to their times. The Constitution, resting in Boston Harbor in America, Nelson's Victory in Portsmouth, England, and the Aurora in Leningrad are three of them. The fourth is HIJMS Mikasa, once the pride of the Imperial Japanese Navy and now firmly anchored, or rather cemented in on Shirahama Beach in Yokosuka, where it has been since November 1926. The site is now called Mikasa Park.

The Mikasa has had several narrow escapes since its construction at the turn of the century by the English company, Vickers. Damaged during the early skirmishes of the Russo-Japanese war (1904-05), it underwent repairs before completing that war in victorious fashion, leading the destruction of the Russian fleet in the Battle of the Japan Sea in May 1905.

After World War II, the Occupation forces saw the Mikasa as a symbol of Japanese imperial militarism and therefore, in line with the policy of demilitarizing Japan, disarmed the ship, which was subsequently left to a rusty existence, forgotten by most people. The problem of what to do with the Mikasa found one solution when the private Japanese organization entrusted with its custody converted the inside into a dance-hall and marked its future as a cabaret.

It was then that a public campaign began to preserve the ship. The Mikasa Preservation Society was organized in 1958 and the ship restored to its original condition at a cost of ¥180 million. It was reopened to the public on May 27, 1961, the 56th anniversary of the Battle of the Japan Sea, the victory which signaled the emerging strength of Asia and which pushed Russia a step nearer to revolution.

Included in the exhibition are a number of models, paintings and photographs of the period, together with a large collection of medals, uniforms and other relics: the white tablecloth with which the Russian destroyer Vedowy surrendered in May 1905; the bell of the Mikasa, cracked and scarred by shell-fire; a letter of victory congratulations from the British Navy; a letter from President Roosevelt commending the leadership of Adm. Togo; photographs of the young crew down on their knees scrubbing the deck, or taking their 15-minute break for a smoke, and various other pointers to what life must have been like on board the ship. And in contrast to the crew's quarters, with hardly enough room to swing a hammock, there are the relatively spacious, hotel-like quarters of the commander.

The Mikasa was the flagship of Adm. Togo (1847-1934) and as such the display contains much relating to the life of the famous leader, including his handprint. There is a statue of Togo in front of the battleship.

A good view of the battleship can be obtained by taking the ferry out into the bay. The ferry actually visits the small Sarushima Isle, about one kilometer from the shore. Until 1945, this isle was a fortified area, but now it is a peaceful natural park with many kinds of subtropical plants and several ideal picnic spots.

Mikasa Park is situated a 10-minute walk from Yokosuka Chuo Station on the Keihin Kyuko Line, about 50 minutes from Shinagawa. Turn left out of the station and follow the main road to a junction, where a sign directs you to the park.

Park With an Int'l Flavor

UNESCO Village   ユネスコ村

The fact that Japan became affiliated with the United Nations Educational, Scientific and Cultural Organization in 1951 does not appear to be the subject of a leisure topic. To mark that occasion, however, Seibu Railway Company planned and constructed a park of traditional dwellings from around the world. Called UNESCO Village and situated on the southeast shore of Sayama Lake, the park has become a regular on the calendar of outings for schoolchildren.

Sayama Lake, otherwise known as Yamaguchi Reservoir which was completed in 1934, has lent its name to what is known as Sayama Natural Park, comprising the huge Seibuen amusement park at one end and UNESCO Village at the other. They are connected by a delightful miniature train which winds its way past the Sayama Golf Course and the Sayama Indoor Skiing Ground to join the two recreation spots in about 10 minutes (fare ¥200).

UNESCO Village is a wooded park of low hills, rising and dipping to hide the 43 native dwellings of the countries which were members of UNESCO when Japan joined. Starting from the east entrance, where a small lake lies under "Spectacle Bridge," four totem poles rise colorfully to greet visitors.

The steps leading up from the totem pole gate enter the Fountain Square, with an outdoor stage to the left. The foliage of the surrounding hills hides the small model houses. The first house, immediately to the left of the steps, represents New Zealand and is one of the most attractive on display. At the front are three posts carved with faces, while the rafters and walls are decorated with strikingly simple colors and patterns.

Although some of the houses may be showing signs of wear on

44

the well-trodden study-tourist path, each has its own character in the ever changing environment of the park village. The sandy color of the dome-shaped Syrian dwelling evokes images of the desert, while the thick, horizontal wooden beams of the Norwegian home seem to stand firm against the wind and snow.

The landmark which dominates the whole village is the Dutch windmill, its white rotating shape visible from almost everywhere.

Just beyond the windmill is the modern-looking structure representing Malaysia, which joined UNESCO in June 1958. This building was erected to mark the 20th anniversary of the opening of UNESCO Village and the roof of the two-story wooden structure, pointing sharply into the sky like horns, is said to be typical of dwellings in the southern part of the Malay peninsula.

After making the rounds of this international village, it is a contrast to step back into Japan by visiting Sayamasan Fudoji Temple, located in the southern corner of the park.

The temple itself is a splendid building of the early Edo Period, brought to the site from Ueno in Tokyo, while in its grounds are located several objects designated as having special cultural merit. One of these, at the entrance to the temple, is the Chokugakumon gate, previously located in Jojoji Temple in Tokyo's Minato Ward as the gate to the mausoleum of the second Tokugawa shogun, Hidetada (1578-1632). Much of Jojoji Temple was destroyed in the Tokyo bombings of 1945, but this gate was left, and together with Chojimon gate and the Onarimon gate, found its way to this new park setting.

UNESCO Village is reached by the Seibu lines from Shinjuku or Ikebukuro, getting off at Seibu Kyujomae Station.

Something for Everyone

Hakone Open Air Museum　　　　　　　箱根彫刻の森美術館

The pleasure written all over the faces of young and old alike says it all: there's something for everyone at the Hakone Open Air Museum.

Conceived with the idea of promoting contemporary sculpture as environmental art, Chokoku no Mori ("Forest of Sculpture") is a collection of mainly abstract works set off against green lawns and the surrounding mountains of Hakone National Park. Designed to encourage "a conversation between nature and sculpture," the museum also ensures a conversation between sculpture and man, for many of the exhibits are not here just to be looked at but to be participated in as well.

They range from "My Sky Hole," two cubes — one transparent, one black — linked by an underground passage of wrinkled rubber walls; to "Symphonic Sculpture," a stained glass tower ascended by spiral staircase and commanding a fine view of the whole area; and Carl Milles' soaring "Man and Pegasus," mounted on a white pillar near the entrance.

The open air museum has many works by foreign sculptors, including Henry Moore, whose smooth and graceful "Family Group" has found a home here. Donated by Nelson Rockefeller, it is one of a series in galleries and museums around the world, including the Tate in London and the Museum of Modern Art in New York.

Several of the exhibits have children specifically in mind, such as the "Curved Space Diamond Structure," a fantastic transparent warren teeming with boys and girls.

It is well worth bringing a picnic lunch to the open air museum as

46

there are plenty of places to sit and eat, including the charming Greco Garden, named after the Italian sculptor Emilio Greco, whose works are displayed here. Other outdoor attractions, apart from the beautiful scenery, include a pond and a maze. In the grounds are an art hall and picture gallery.

Admission to the Hakone Open Air Museum costs ¥800 for adults and ¥400 for children.

Hakone Open Air Museum

To reach the museum, take the Odakyu Line from Shinjuku Station to either Odawara or Hakone Yumoto stations. Then transfer to the Hakone Yumoto Tozan railway, which will haul you up through the mountains to Chokoku no Mori Station. From the station it is a short walk.

Zoos, Farms and Leisure Grounds

The big wheel in Tobu Zoo's leisure ground

Not too Much Noise, Please

Ueno Zoo 上野動物園

The star attraction at Ueno Zoo in the last few years has been its pandas. Whether a solitary panda or a pair, these popular animals have invariably drawn flocks of admirers. And in keeping with their status, the zoo has built them a *"mansion,"* complete with double-glazing, airconditioning and concrete beds. At present only Huan Huan is in residence, and an attendant bellows at excited onlookers not to make too much noise as "the poor panda is trying to sleep."

In addition to Huan Huan, Ueno Zoo has more than 8,500 animals comprising nearly 1,000 species. They range in exoticism from the Mikado pheasant and Chinese leopard to the narcissus flycatcher and flying fox.

The zoo is spread over a considerable area, divided into an East and West Garden, and there is a clearly marked course to follow. Dotted along the route are machines with long, elephant-like trunks which for ¥10 give a taped explanation of the birds and beasts. A map of the zoo is available at the entrance.

Within the East Garden is a tea house built more than 300 years ago by Takara Toda, a military commander, and visited by shoguns on their way to nearby Toshogu Shrine.

Crossing from the East Garden to the West, one walks over Aesop's Bridge, not of fabled antiquity but made of concrete. From the bridge there is a fine view across Shinobazu Pond.

Alternatively, Aesop's Bridge may be bypassed for the zoo monorail, Japan's first, which swishes by frequently at ¥100 a trip along a 300-meter track. The monorail terminal in the West Garden is by a children's zoo, where children can look at rabbits and incubating eggs, ride on donkeys and play with geese. Nearby is a display of creatures of the night, which beckons with the words, "Welcome to the World of Darkness."

After all this, there is still the aquarium to be visited, tucked in by Hanazono Gate and charging separate admission. The large tank just inside the entrance always has exciting displays.

Finally, a word on the humans at Ueno: the zoo is very popular, and on holidays and weekends it's sometimes a question of not being able to see the animals for the people.

Ueno Zoo is open from 9:30 a.m. to 4:30 p.m. every day except Monday. Admission costs ¥300 for adults and ¥100 for junior high school students. The over-65s and under-11s get in free.

The monorail at Ueno Zoo

The zoo is located in Ueno Park, a short walk from JNR Ueno and Keisei Ueno stations.

You're Actually Milking a Cow!

Mother Farm   マザー牧場

You take two of the teats of a Holstein in each of your hands and squeeze them gingerly, while a farm milkmaid holds its tail so that it won't hit you in the act. You try two, three, four times, and then suddenly, milk starts spurting in two white lines into the tin bucket underneath. You are actually milking a cow!

This is only one of the many enjoyable activities you can experience on Mother Farm, a 250-hectare tourist farm which lies halfway up picturesque Mt. Kinada in Chiba Prefecture.

After the milking, you may visit the milk plant where they are bottling milk, or the steel silo, the largest one in the Orient, in the Cow Center area. (Be sure to try a bottle of fresh Mother Farm milk afterward).

At Livestock Square in the central part of the farm, you are free to play with calves, cuddle rabbits or feed goats with grass. Adjacent to the square there is the Festival Plaza where you can join in an amusing pig race, pairing with one of the little pigs, or watch sheep marching across accompanied by a sheep dog.

As no agricultural chemicals are used on the farm, it is a good place to take children for hunting insects in the summer. The Shizen Kansatsu-en (Park for Nature Study), which stretches out to the left from the main gate, is 10 times as large as Korakuen Stadium and is the home of grasshoppers, beetles and cicadas, as well as various kinds of birds.

·The best seasons to visit the farm are spring and autumn when the weather is mild. In spring you can enjoy strawberry picking, potato digging and the Nanohana Flower Festival, and in autumn, sweetpotato digging and the Scarecrow Festival featuring 100 humorous scarecrows.

As well as the farm and pastoral attractions, there is Nihon Jido Kaikan, a museum displaying Japanese picture books and folk toys. The building, with an observatory on top, is located on a hill near Livestock Square.

For those who would like to meditate in the vast stretch of pastoral beauty, there is the Kokusai Zen Dojo (International Zen Seminary) on the far side of the farm.

Ending the eventful day with an outside barbecue would be a good idea. The farm serves *"kinada-yaki,"* a barbecue course of trout, chicken and vegetables, outside. Also in the Genghis Khan Center, Mongolian mutton (or beef) barbecue courses are served.

Opening hours are from 8 a.m. to 5 p.m. (8 a.m. to 9 p.m. in July and August). The farm is closed on the second Tuesday of each month in June and July, and every Tuesday from December to February. Entrance costs ¥600 for adults, ¥300 for children.

For further information, including the hours for milking demonstrations and the pig races, call Mother Farm, 0439-37-3211, or the Mother Farm Tokyo Information Office, (03) 431-7241.

To reach Mother Farm, take the bus bound for Mt. Kano which stops at the farm (25 min.) from Sanukimachi Station on the Uchibo Line (one-and-a-half hours from Tokyo by express).

Don't Worry, It's Only a Goat...

Children's Zoos   牧ガ原公園／子ども動物自然公園

"Don't be frightened, it's only a goat," says the mother, but still the child hesitates before thrusting its gift of weeds toward the animal.

Most zoos are populated by elephants, lions, tigers and other such captured animals which children can only gaze at as they would a picture book. Such a zoo probably does a lot to increase a child's knowledge of distant animals, but not much to increase feelings of intimacy with nature.

Recently a growing interest has been seen in another kind of zoo, featuring not wild animals, but farm animals which children can approach, touch and even play with. One of these is the Children's Zoo (Chibikko Dobutsuen), located in **Makigahara Park** near Yokohama.

The farm zoo is situated inside the park just beyond the large pond, which is always circled by young boys and adults trying their hand at fishing. The zoo is nicely set out in a rural manner, and the animals are kept in pens. The ponies, goats and cows seem to show the greatest interest in their visitors, and to draw the most attention. The pigs and sheep mind their own business.

Other animals include rabbits — which all appear to hide from the staring eyes — guinea pigs, turtles and swans, and there is an aviary with various kinds of birds. The farm zoo is kept clean and tidy, and, judging by the many smiling faces, is very popular with young visitors.

The park itself covers a much larger area, with the hills around it offering excellent space for strolls and picnics in the cherry blossom forest. There is also a fine play-ground area, called the "Toride no

Mori," giving children — and adults, too — a challenging time finding their way around a tasking course of log walls, bridges, swinging ropes and slides.

The Makigahara Children's Zoo Park is a pleasant and healthy place. Entrance is free, and the zoo is open from 9 a.m. to 4:30 p.m., being closed on Mondays.

Another children's zoo is the **Kodomo Dobutsu Shizen Koen** (Children's Animal Nature Park) in Saitama. Opened in 1980 — on Children's Day, aptly enough — the park claims to be the largest of its kind in Japan. It is located in a wide green area of hills, forests, ponds and small rivers.

Here also it is possible for children to come into contact with a variety of mainly herbivorous animals. In a friends' corner, they are invited to touch and play with rabbits, goats, squirrels and a number of other pets. Altogether there are said to be over 440 animals of some 50 types in the zoo, all ready to welcome young visitors.

Other areas in the zoo park include a pony corner, where children can take rides, a horseriding corner, a flamingo corner, a natural education corner, where children can observe cows being milked, and, just to round it all off, a model monster corner.

This zoo park is open from 9:30 a.m. to 5 p.m. and closed on Mondays. Entrance is ¥300 for senior high school students and above, ¥100 for junior high and elementary school pupils, and free for children under 6 years of age.

Makigahara Children's Zoo Park is located a 5-minute bus ride from Futamatagawa Station on the Sotetsu Line which leaves Yokohama Station.

Kodomo Dobutsu Shizen Koen is located a 10-minute bus ride from Takasaka Station on the Tobu Tojo Line.

New Home for Lucky the Lion

Tobu Zoological Park   東武動物園

Lucky the lion, for one, must have been glad that the Tobu Zoological Park was opened in the spring of 1981.

The pet of a private owner living in Saitama, Lucky was handed down the death sentence by the prefectural government as a result of his violent character which caused him to attack and wound visitors to his house on at least two occasions.

A 4-year-old, weighing 300 kg at the time, Lucky was saved by an appeal from his owner and eventually the willingness of Tobu Zoo to take him in. And there he now lives, with a large cage all his own and a prominent and appropriate sign — "I'm Lucky"! No doubt his former neighbors are thinking the same.

Planned to commemorate the 80th anniversary of the founding of the Tobu Railway Company, the zoo took three years to complete. In charge is Toshio Nishiyama, "Uncle Hippo" to those who know him, because of his experience in charge of the hippos at Ueno Zoo and because, apparently, he bears a striking resemblance to his thick-skinned wards.

Now Nishiyama takes care of not only hippos, but over 300 other types of animals as well, and he has an area of land about four times the size of Ueno Zoo on which to do so. Originally, plans were to have a safari-type zoo park, rather like Tama Zoo with its lion-viewing buses, but the unsuitability of the land forced a change to a more conventional type.

Zoos have come a long way in recent years, and are no longer just exhibitions of strange animals in museums. Indeed, Tobu Zoo shares its site with a *yuenchi* amusement park on the eastern side and a *bokujo* pasture zone on the west. And a prerequisite of all zoos these days, not forgotten at Tobu, is a small area set aside for children to make contact with the more pacific of our animal friends, like donkeys, ponies and so on.

The advice given is to visit the amusement park first, as by afternoon, especially on weekends, queues for the big wheel and other attractions can mean as much as a one-hour wait.

As well as Lucky, popular crowd-pullers seem to be the African area; the monkey house which includes among others the black spider monkey, the pig-tailed monkey and the crab-eating monkey; the Australian prairie area, and the alpaca, an animal from Peru related to the camel and resembling a llama, which is making its first appearance in Japan.

Also found in the central area, near the children's zoo, is a Small Animals Center housing a raccoon dog, porcupines and so on, and in the western area, together with the pasture zone, there is a bird park. A boating lake, outdoor stage and various kiosks complete the facilities available.

While copying the commercialism so often seen at large leisure facilities in Japan, Tobu Zoological Park also provides much to catch the interest of both young and adult visitors. Entrance is ¥1,000 for all over junior high school-age and ¥500 for children over 4.

Hours are 9:30 a.m.-5:45 p.m. (from 10 a.m. on weekdays) between March 21 and Sept. 20, and 10 a.m.-4 p.m. all days between Sept. 21 and March 20. The zoo park is closed on Mondays, except for the March 21-May 31, July 21-Aug. 31 and Oct. 1-31 periods, and Dec. 28-Jan. 2.

The best way to reach Tobu Zoo is by the Tobu Isezaki Line from Kita Senju, getting off at what used to be Sugito Station, but is now Tobu Dobutsu Koen Station. The Hibiya subway line also runs through to this station, from where the park's big Ferris wheel can be seen.

Bigger, Higher and Faster

Leisure Grounds   花やしき遊園地ほか

The pleasure ground as we know it today, a fixed spot of permanent fun and excitement, first became popular in Japan in the 1920s, and the private railway companies were in the thick of it.

As private railway lines began to sprout up around the big cities of Tokyo and Osaka, so also the amusement grounds began to appear: Tamagawaen in 1925 (Tokyu), Mukogaoka in 1926 (Odakyu), and Toshimaen (Seibu) the same year.

Others followed after the war as the demand for leisure facilities grew. Korakuen opened in 1955, and Yomiuri Land in 1964, the latter managed by the same company which created Nara Dreamland, an amusement park modeled after Disneyland in America.

And, whether to satisfy the appetites of a thrill-thirsty public or simply to outdo their rivals, the scale of the excitement — some might say the risk — involved has rocketed. So that's how we've come to get the Watershoots and the Loop Coasters and the Boomerangs, the Shuttle Loops and the Wonder Wheels.

Fortunately, for those wishing to look but not daring to try these bigger machines, all the amusement grounds still continue more down-to-earth entertainment such as merry-go-rounds, minitrains, shooting ranges and game centers.

One of the best places to begin is Hanayashiki Yuenchi in Asakusa, which is also a fitting start because the history of Japan's amusement grounds very much goes back to outside entertainment of the Edo Period, and Hanayashiki was one such place popular for puppet shows, monkey performances, haunted house entertainment and so on.

The Hanayashiki site was destroyed in the Kanto Earthquake, but started life again as an amusement park after the war. In terms of size, it is comparatively small in scale, and because of this, and perhaps also the fact that it is situated behind Asakusa Temple, a large number of young children and elderly people can be seen enjoying its facilities, which include a modest jet coaster, ghost train, various shooting ranges and a Panorama Hall with scenes of old Asakusa.

The great attraction of Hanayashiki is that entrance is free. Once inside, tickets can be purchased for rides on the various facilities, costing from ¥100 to ¥300. It is open from 10 a.m. to 6 p.m. and closed on Fridays. Get off the subway at Asakusa, take Nakamise Street up to the temple, then follow Hanayashiki Street to the colorful entrance.

Following is information on the other main amusement grounds in the Tokyo area. Please remember that entrance fees and opening times are subject to change.

Korakuen in Bunkyo Ward, Tokyo, with its Skyflower. Adults ¥800, children ¥500. Open 10 a.m. to 7 p.m. Closed on Mondays. Tel.: (03) 811-2111. From Korakuen Station on Marunouchi subway line or JNR Sobu Line's Suidobashi Station.

Toshimaen in Nerima Ward, with its Corkscrew Coaster. Adults ¥1,000, children ¥500. Open 9 a.m. to 5 p.m. No holidays. Tel: (03) 990-3131. From Toshimaen Station on Seibu Ikebukuro Line.

Seibuen in Tokorozawa, with UNESCO Village nearby. Adults ¥800, children ¥500. Open 9:30 a.m. to 5 p.m. No holidays. Tel: (0429) 22-1371. From Seibu Yuenchi Station on Seibu Shinjuku Line.

Mukogaoka Yuen in Kawasaki, with its monorail link. Adults ¥700, children ¥400. Open 9 a.m. to 5 p.m. No holidays. Tel.:(044) 911-4281. From Mukogaoka Yuen Station on the Odakyu Line.

Futakotamagawaen in Setagaya Ward, Tokyo, an amusement ground particularly suited for children. Adults ¥600, children ¥300. Open 9 a.m. to 5 p.m. No holidays. Tel.: (03) 700-0061. From

Futakotamagawaen Station on Shin Tamagawa and Oimachi lines.

Yomiuri Land in Kawasaki, with what is said to be the biggest Big Wheel in the world. Adults ¥800, children ¥400. Open 10 a.m. (9 a.m. on school holidays) to 5 p.m. Closed on Tuesdays. Tel.:(044) 966-1111. From Yomiuri Land-mae Station on the Odakyu Line.

Yokohama Dreamland, with its Shuttle Loop and Wonder Wheel. Adults ¥1,500, high school students ¥1,000, children ¥700. On weekdays, ¥1,200, ¥1,000 and ¥600 respectively. Open from 10 a.m. to 5:30 p.m. No holidays. Tel.:(045) 851-1411. From JNR Ofuna Station.

Tama Tech in Hino City, which provides a good day out when combined with Tama Zoo. Adults ¥800, children ¥400. Open 9 a.m. to 5:15 p.m. (from 9:30 on weekdays). No holidays. Tel: (0425) 91-0820. Five minutes by bus from Tama Dobutsukoen Station on the Keio Line.

Going a little further afield, there are also large amusement parks in Shizuoka (Nippon Land and Gotenba Family Land), Tochigi (Oyama Yuenchi), Kanagawa (Sagamiko Picnic Land), Akigawa City (Tokyo Summerland), and Yamanashi (Fujikyu Highland).

Once inside the amusement grounds, you will find that entertainment facilities cost about ¥100-400 per ride. On a smaller and cheaper scale, don't forget that mini pleasure grounds can often be found in the corners of large parks or even on the roofs of some department stores.

Temples, Shrines and Cathedrals

Tsukiji Honganji Temple

Nine Buddhas in Paradise

Kuhonbutsu   九品仏

As far as the layman is concerned, Buddhist images are a bit like the temples in which they are found. Both tend to look like small replicas of the bigger and more famous survivors in Kamakura and Kyoto. The images, moreover, usually have the pose and beauty of spiritual qualities which we laymen can marvel at but never grasp.

The expression of peaceful bliss, wisdom and mercy characterizing most typical Buddhist images hides the fact that there are actually a variety of types, and closer scrutiny reveals differences.

Close scrutiny is certainly necessary when viewing the nine statues of Amida-Nyorai Buddha at Joshinji Temple, better known as Kuhonbutsu, located near Jiyugaoka in Tokyo's Setagaya Ward. This temple was built in 1678 as a branch temple of Zojoji Temple in Shiba Park, Tokyo. That was the time of the fourth Tokugawa shogunate and the story goes that the temple near Jiyugaoka was built on the orders of a priest called Kaseki, who lived from 1617 until 1694.

Like its parent temple in Shiba, Joshinji Temple belongs to the Jodo sect of Buddhism, a sect with roots going back to the Kamakura Period of Japanese history. The sect was founded in 1175 by a priest called Honen. That particularly turbulent period of history saw the emergence of several sects of Buddhism and the Jodo sect gained considerable popularity, it is said, apparently because it placed emphasis on faith and belief rather than on intellectual understanding.

And that was where the priest Kaseki came in, for he was also famous as a sculptor and spent 33 years, from the age of 18 until 51, on what may be called his life work, the sculpting of nine images of

Amida Buddha. Having completed them, he wanted to protect them from the danger of floods, and so moved them inland to the Joshinji Temple setting, previously the site of Okusawa Castle.

And indeed, they have survived until the present, all nine of them, and the area is known as Kuhonbutsu, the nine Buddhas in paradise.

It is claimed, perhaps rather exaggeratedly, that the appearance of the area has scarcely changed since the temple was first established. With its thatched roofing, the gate at the entrance certainly introduces a rural atmosphere to the setting. Inside the gate and to the left is a garden called the Heron Garden, a small area of plants and trees. Indeed, the whole area was once called Heron Valley.

Straight ahead is the Niomon, the Deva Gate of the temple with its thick pillars housing the two guardian gods of the temple. These somewhat ferocious looking statues are traditionally placed at the entrance to temples to keep away evil spirits.

Passing through this gate, to the left is the elegant-looking bell tower, built in 1708, and to the right is the main building of the temple. All these structures had thatched roofs, as the entrance gate still does, until 1965, when they underwent repairs and the roofs were replaced. The atmosphere of age, however, is protected by the magnificent trees in the grounds. In particular, the huge and dominating nutmeg tree, 31 meters high, is said to be the biggest in Tokyo, and there is an equally handsome gingko tree with a height of 18 meters.

And on the far side of the temple grounds are the three halls with the famous nine gilded images of Buddha. Unfortunately, in the darkness it is not so easy to see them, but each one has different expressions, poses and positioning of the hands. According to the doctrine of the Jodo sect, the basis of Buddhism is having belief in the saving power of Amida Buddha and through belief, rebirth is promised in the Pure Land (Jodo).

Take the Toyoko Line from Shibuya to Jiyugaoka and change onto the Denentoshi Line. The next stop is Kuhonbutsu Station. Leaving the station, turn left over the railway and a long, narrow, tree-lined path leads up to the entrance of the temple grounds.

Shrine Engulfed by Sports Mecca

Hikawa Shrine   氷川神社（埼玉・大宮）

While most people take their prayers to the local shrine or temple at New Year's, others go farther afield to more famous places such as Meiji Jingu Shrine. There are, of course, many splendid shrines to visit, and included in their number is Hikawa Shrine in Omiya.

One record has the shrine dating from 473 B.C., although its history seems to be uncertain. There were originally three shrines situated on the edge of Minuma Marsh, which extended around the area now occupied by Urawa and Omiya. The marshland was reclaimed during the Edo Period, and it was after the Meiji Restoration that the three small shrines were combined to form Hikawa Shrine.

The buildings have undergone restoration work several times, once having been reconstructed by Minamoto Yoritomo in 1180. The present buildings date from the beginning of the Showa Period, and the main hall was reconstructed in 1940.

Hikawa Shrine, with its fine tower gate, pond and extensive area, has a quiet and reclusive atmosphere which is made even more noticeable by its location among the cedars in a corner of Omiya Park.

Actually it was the shrine which came first. The park was opened to the north of it in 1884, but now is the dominant partner with its athletic stadium, baseball park, tennis courts and bicycle race track. These facilities, which are the reason why the park is called Saitama Prefecture's sports mecca, spill over into the greenery itself, for the park also has a 1,500-meter jogging course, and a track-suited runner emerging from the distance is no unusual sight.

As well as its sports facilities, the park also has many attractions for children. Apart from the wide open areas themselves, there is a boating lake, a play area of swings and other amusements, and a small zoo, the location of which can easily be determined from the noisy but cheerful sounds of the animals.

There is also a cultural side to the park. It isn't open on New Year's Day, but the Saitama Prefectural Museum is located among the pine trees in the western part near the lake. The museum was opened in 1971 to commemorate the 100th anniversary of Saitama's designation as a prefecture, and it exhibits various artifacts of Saitama life and history, as well as an art display.

To the north of the park, across the railway line, is Omiya Bonsai Village, which with the recent *bonsai* boom has become a well-known tourist spot in itself. The village was set up after several people in the *bonsai* business moved to the area after the Great Kanto Earthquake in 1923. Now various kinds of *bonsai* plants are displayed and sold there.

And nearby the *bonsai* village is the Omiya Manga (Cartoon) Kaikan, located in a small building which was the residence of Kitazawa Rakuten (1876-1955), who has been called the founder of the modern cartoon in Japan. On the first floor there is a display on Kitazawa Rakuten himself, and the second floor is devoted to modern cartoons. The cartoon museum is open from 9 to 4 p.m. and closed on Mondays and national holidays. Entrance is free.

Hikawa Shrine and Omiya Park are best reached from Omiya Koen Station on the Tobu Noda Line from JNR's Omiya Station. They are situated a five-minute walk from the station.

The Spirit of Musashino

Heirinji 平林寺

There are two places in Saitama going by the name of Heirinji. One is situated near the old doll town of Iwatsuki, just to the east of Omiya, and the other further west, in the city of Niiza. It is the latter which indicates the location of the well-known Heirinji Temple, but the former is not without relevance, because it was in Iwatsuki that the temple was originally built some 600 years ago, in 1375.

The temple, apparently destroyed in the 16th century, was rebuilt at its present site as the family temple of Matsudaira Nobutsuna, *daimyo* of nearby Kawagoe and supporter of the Tokugawa shogunate. Nobutsuna died in 1662, and work on the temple was brought to completion the following year by his son Terutsuna. Nobutsuna had already made his mark on the area by having an irrigation ditch constructed to bring water to the district. A branch stream of this runs through the temple grounds.

The western side of Tokyo has now been thoroughly urbanized, but in centuries past, when Edo was but a small village, it consisted of the great plain of Musashino. There are still many spots which are said to retain the old rural atmosphere of Musashino with its densely wooded areas, but in none is the spirit so well preserved as it is in Heirinji.

It is a remote place, and the bus seems to drop you off in the middle of nowhere. Once through the entrance gate and among the thatched roofs and green foliage, however, there's no turning back. Immediately in front of you is the main *sanmon* temple gate, the original structure still standing. The *nio* statues on either side of the gate are said to have been carved by Unkei (1148-1223), the sculptor responsible for many great works, including statues of Buddha at Todaiji and Kofukuji temples in Nara.

Inside the gate are the main buildings of the Rinzai Sect temple and an inner garden, while to the left there is a small lake. The path going round this leads off into the wooded area behind the temple. The area is open all year round, but visits toward the end of the year for the autumn foliage and in spring for the plum and cherry blossom seasons are particularly rewarding. Being one of the few remaining Musashino woodland spots, the area here is also famous for its wild birds, and there are said to be about 60 species making their homes around the temple.

Also located around the temple grounds are some 170 gravestones, including those of Nobutsuna and his wife, and other temple buildings, shrines and stone lanterns. The area is designated as a natural monument and the route around it takes well over an hour to complete at a leisurely pace, bringing you back eventually to the temple gate. The grounds are open from 9 a.m. to 4 p.m. and entrance is ¥200.

Heirinji bus stop for the temple is served by No. 73 bus running between Hibarigaoka Station on the Seibu Ikebukuro Line and Shiki Station on the Tobu Tojo Line and the No. 22 bus from Higashi-kurume Station on the Seibu Ikebukuro Line bound for Asakasumidai. Both buses run rather infrequently.

Some Eye-Catching Structures

Cathedrals   ニコライ堂ほか

One of the more unexpected sights in Tokyo is a large Hindu-style temple, the Tsukiji Honganji, a branch of the Nishi Honganji temple in Kyoto. The present eye-catching structure was completed in 1934, replacing an earlier building razed to the ground by fire following the Great Kanto Earthquake of 1923.

Tsukiji Honganji is built upon reclaimed land, or *"tsukiji,"* from which the name derives. When the original temple, dating from 1617, was destroyed by fire in 1657, the Tokugawa shogunate granted the Buddhist sect a large tract of submerged land along the shore of Tokyo Bay, provided the temple did the work of reclamation itself. This was done with the help of priests and parishoners, and a temple has existed on the site ever since.

Tsukiji Honganji's roomy interior, its roof supported by great white pillars, has seating for upward of 1,000 people. An unusual feature for a Buddhist temple is the large organ located at the rear of the main hall of worship. Organ recitals are held about once every two months.

The biggest organ in use in a Japanese church, however, is to be found across Tokyo in St. Mary's Cathedral. The cathedral, designed by Kenzo Tange (who also designed the National Indoor Stadium for the 1964 Tokyo Olympics), is as striking from the outside as from within. The exterior is made of dazzling stainless steel. Standing independently, and visible from afar, is a bell tower, topped off by a cross that soars more than 60 meters high.

Inside the cathedral, which was completed in 1964, the pre-cast concrete walls are many shades of grey. There are no stained-glass windows, but at the back of the cross is a glowing plate of dappled marble allowing soft light to fall on the altar. On display is a papal seat used by Pope John Paul II when he visited St. Mary's in February 1981. The cathedral seats 600 and has standing room for 2,000.

Another cathedral in Tokyo is to be found near Ochanomizu Station. This is the Nicolai Cathedral of the Greek Orthodox Church, named after its founder, the Russian priest Ioan Kasatkin Nicolai (1836-1912).

Work on the cathedral began in 1884, and was completed about seven years later in 1891. The Byzantine-style cathedral was designed by a Russian, and its construction supervised by an Englishman. The cathedral is topped off by a large dome that stands 35 meters high. There are many icons inside, some dating back to the 18th century.

The cathedral was extensively damaged in the Great Kanto Earthquake, but by 1929 it had been completely repaired.

Tsukiji Honganji and St. Mary's Cathedral are open daily to visitors. The Nicolai Cathedral is open to the public between 1 p.m. and 4 p.m. from Tuesdays to Saturdays. On Sunday it is open all day. In addition, all have regularly scheduled services, and a trip to hear the Nicolai Cathedral choir is highly recommended.

Tsukiji Honganji is located by Tsukiji Station on the Hibiya subway line. St. Mary's Cathedral is a 20-minute walk from Mejiro Station on the Yamanote Line. Leaving the station, turn right and follow the main road. Or take a number 61 bus bound for Shinjuku Nishi-Guchi, alighting at Sekiguchi San-chome. The cathedral is opposite the Chinzanso Restaurant. The Nicolai Cathedral is a five-minute walk from Ochanomizu Station on the Chuo Line.

Historical Routes

Yokohama street tiles

City's Last Tram Rattles On

Arakawa Line Tram　　　　　　　　都電荒川線

The Arakawa Line tram, the city's last, carries its passengers on an intimate journey across Tokyo. The smart yellow-and-blue cars cut between back gardens, pass by temples and shrines, stop at toy town-size stations and thread their way across busy intersections, dutifully waiting at red lights just like any other road user.

There are altogether 29 stops along the way, starting at Waseda, near the university, and ending at Minowa, in Tokyo's *shitamachi* (downtown). The tram passes through four city wards — Shinjuku, Toshima, Kita and Arakawa. A journey from end to end without alighting takes 50 minutes, but there are many places of interest en route, and a handy little map (in Japanese) available free of charge shows just where these are.

Before boarding the one-man tram, visit Waseda University and the theater museum, built in 1928 in honor of dramatist Dr. Shoyo Tsubouchi who translated the complete works of Shakespeare into Japanese. The museum contains many exhibits connected with the theater, and is open daily except Sundays.

Next are two pleasant gardens. Shin Edogawa Garden is a short walk from the Waseda terminus, on the far side of the nearby Kanda River. Kansenen Park, noted for the clear waters of its spring, lies between Waseda and Omokagebashi. Several stops on is Kishibojin, a shrine for pregnant women and in its grounds a gingko tree said to be more than 600 years old.

Leaving Kishibojin behind, the tram rattles on, passing very close to the Sunshine 60 building in Ikebukuro before ducking under the Yamanote Line at Otsuka Station.

The stop at Asukayama is right across the street from the noted cherry blossom park of the same name. The park is long and narrow, and has a splendid fountain. A fair detour from the tram, walking up Hongo Dori leaving Asukayama Park on the left, is Furukawa Garden. The grounds contain an Edwardian-style house surrounded by lawns, flowerbeds and well-kept hedges, side by side with a Japanese-style garden. The house once belonged to Ichibei Furukawa (1832-1903), a mining industrialist. The garden is a 15-20 minute walk from Asukayama.

By Oji Station-mae, the next stop and halfway point of the ride, is a Kami no Hakubutsukan (Paper Museum), said to be the only one of its kind in the world. The museum shows how paper is made, the uses — utilitarian and artistic — to which it is put, and contains a reference library. A 10-minute walk from the station is Nanushi-no-taki, a garden which takes its name from one of the waterfalls within its walls.

Back on the tram, and more parks come into range. The Arakawa amusement park, situated on the banks of the Arakawa River, is near Nishi Oku Nana, and two stops from the end of the line — alight at Arakawa Ni — is the Arakawa Natural Park, looking anything but natural and located by a sewage works.

Nearest stations are Takadanobaba on the Yamanote Line for the tram's Waseda terminus, and Minowa on the Hibiya subway line for Minowa. The trams run very frequently, and cost ¥120 per ride. A ¥600 one-day pass is available.

Remembering Yokohama's Sons

Yokohama I 横浜 I

Much of the history of Yokohama over the last century or so relates to the arrival of foreigners and their subsequent contributions to the city and the country. You can't go very far without coming across some kind of monument to a foreign "son of Yokohama," and of course the Foreigners' Cemetery is full of the names of foreigners who lived and died in this country.

Located in a corner of Minato no Mieru Oka Park, however, is a museum dedicated to one of the Japanese sons of Yokohama, Jiro Osaragi. The author of over 500 books, and many other articles, plays and poems, Osaragi was born in Yokohama in 1897. His writing career began after he graduated from Tokyo University in 1922, and his "Homecoming" won a Japan Art Academy award in 1950. Many of his works have been translated and made into movies.

Osaragi died of cancer in 1973, and the memorial museum was opened in 1978 displaying the many valuable belongings which he left and reflecting the great activity which characterized his career. The red-brick building has a French look about it, including a salon on the second floor, and this is not surprising since much of Osaragi's non-fictional interest lay in France.

His first non-fiction work, published in 1930, was on the Dreyfus affair, and in 1961, at the age of 64, he visited France, gathering materials and finally writing a book on the Paris Commune.

The Jiro Osaragi Memorial Museum is open from 10 a.m. until 5:30 p.m. (until 5 p.m. from October to March), and the entrance fee is ¥150 for adults and ¥50 for children. It is easily reached from the south exit of Ishikawacho Station. Turn right and follow the

74

fashionable Motomachi shopping street to the end before branching off and up to the right, the hill leading to the Foreigners' Cemetery, which unfortunately is not open to the public. Nearby is the Meiji-Period Yamate Museum.

From here take the road to the left, past the spot where the old Gaiety Theater, built in 1885 by foreigners and a great influence on Japanese theater, used to be, and you come to the park's entrance. Just to the right is the English Mansion, which was the official residence of the British consul-general. Unfortunately, only the garden is accessible to the public.

Inside the park, which was once the site of the English barracks, there is a fine view of Yokohama Port. To the right is the Osaragi Memorial Museum, and beyond that the southern part of the park. The Minato no Mieru Oka Park was opened as such in 1962, and in 1971 the French Hill part was added, this having been the place where French troops were garrisoned at the time of the opening of the port.

Leaving the Minato no Mieru Oka Park from the French Hill side, it is just a short walk to Marine Tower. On the way, in front of the Yokohama District Consolidated Administration Office, there is a monument at the spot where another of Yokohama's "sons," Dr. James Hepburn, lived from 1862 until 1875. The monument was erected in 1949 to mark the 90th anniversary of Hepburn's first arrival in Japan.

Hepburn, perhaps most famous for his contributions to Romanizing Japanese, first came to Japan as a missionary. He lived for three years at Jyobutsuji Temple in Kanagawa before moving to Yokohama, and included in his work was a translation of the Bible into Japanese, the completion of a Japanese-English dictionary and the dissemination of Western medical science.

The Marine Tower itself was completed in 1961 in commemoration of the centennial anniversary of Yokohama's opening to foreign trade in 1859. It is 106 meters high with many facilities, including an observation platform and a Marine Science Museum on the third floor. Entrance to the tower is ¥600 for adults,

¥300 for high school students and ¥200 for children.

After the tower and a short rest in Yamashita Park across the road, the best way to return is to walk back inland to Yokohama's famous Chinatown, a long street of Chinese-style shops and restaurants which Chinese residents of the area have kept going since the early Meiji Period despite its being destroyed by the Great Kanto Earthquake and again by bombings in World War II.

Yamashita Park and Yokohama Port

Monuments, Museums and More

Yokohama II

Yokohama was opened up as a port on June 2, 1859, and the city is full of monuments commemorating that landmark period in the area's history. Celebration of the day itself, however, is annually brought forward one month to May 3, the weather in June being so unreliable. The most famous of the many events taking place on this occasion is the International Fancy Dress Parade, which usually starts from in front of the Chamber of Commerce and Industry on Nihon Odori.

For those wishing to see the colorful events of the Port Festival and take in something of the history of Yokohama at the same time, a good place to start is the north exit of Kannai Station on the JNR Keihin Tohoku Line. Take the exit to the right, and walk along parallel to the railway line until you reach Basha Michi, easily recognizable by its green lampposts, telephone boxes, benches and brick paving.

Foreigners who came to Yokohama after 1859 brought with them their horse-drawn carriages, and the sight of them riding around the city is said to have intrigued the local citizens. The traffic of one- or two-horse carriages became so congested that the busy route from Honmachi-dori to Yoshida-bashi was widened in 1867, creating the Basha Michi which remains today.

Noting that the Japanese found the horse and carriage so intriguing, some foreigners went on to form a company operating a return run between Yokohama and Tokyo, and when in 1869 a Japanese, Renjo Shimooka, created a rival company, the race was on. At that time, a carriage drawn by two horses and carrying six people would cover the one-way distance in some four hours.

The walk along Basha Michi brings you to the imposing Prefectural Museum on the left, at the junction with Benten Street. The building, previously the head office of a bank, was constructed in 1904, and is said to be one of the most representative of Meiji structures remaining in Yokohama. Turned into a museum in 1967, the German-Renaissance style building, with its prominent dome, contains a wide variety of exhibits of archaeological, geographical and historical interest. It is open from 9 a.m. to 4:30 p.m., closed on Mondays, and entrance is ¥200 for adults and ¥50 for children.

Walking past the museum, turn right at Honmachi Street and keep going until you reach the Port-Opening Memorial Hall (Kaiko Kinenkan) on the right. Yokohama is a city of monuments, and in front of this splendid building are three of them. One marks the site of the former town administration which conducted Yokohama's affairs from 1868-89, when the town became a municipality. From 1859-68, a large silk dealer had its headquarters there, managed by the father of Tenshin Okakura, who appears in one other of the three monuments.

Okakura was born at this site in 1862 and lived in Yokohama until he was 12. Famous as a promoter of fine arts, he became head of the Tokyo School of Fine Arts at the age of 29, and he did much to introduce Japanese fine arts to the West, visiting India and the United States, where he became chief curator of Oriental fine arts at the Boston Museum. The other monument commemorates the Chamber of Commerce, which was set up at the site in 1880.

From here Honmachi Street passes the Kanagawa Prefectural Office and meets Nihon Odori street, where the annual fancy dress parade starts from. On the corner there is a monument commemorating the Kanagawa Maritime Transportation Office which was established here at the time of the opening of the port to deal with customs and diplomatic affairs.

While walking around Yokohama, it's a good idea to keep your eyes on the ground occasionally, because the pavements are set with illustrated tiles showing various aspects of the history and life of Yokohama and they lead you around the city in a colorful way.

78

The next stop is a monument at the site where the Japan-America Treaty of Amity and Friendship was concluded, and across the road from this is the Silk Center, with the Silk Museum on the second floor. The Silk Center was set up in 1959 to commemorate the centennial anniversary of the opening of the Port of Yokohama. The museum has many costumes on display, including Yokohama scarves, and also explains how silk is produced and how the opening of the port and the growth of the silk industry went together.

The museum is open from 9 a.m. to 4:30 p.m. and closed only at year's end. Entrance is ¥300 for adults, ¥200 for students and ¥100 for junior high and elementary pupils. Outside is the well-known statue of the girl with silk, and by this is a monument marking the site where the first foreign trading house, called the Ei-Ichiban Kan (First English House) was located after the opening of the port.

Across the street and facing the bay is Yamashita Park, in the far corner of which is perhaps Yokohama's biggest and most famous monument, the Hikawa Maru, which is moored near the shore and open to the public. Built in 1930, the liner crossed the Pacific 238 times up to 1960 on the North American passage. For these who like exploring ships, entrance is ¥600 for senior high school students and above, ¥300 for children above 6, and ¥200 for infants.

Hiking Trails Around Kamakura

Kamakura 鎌倉

First time visitors to Kamakura probably have the Great Buddha and Hachimangu Shrine at the top of their list of "musts." But this historically important city, surrounded on three sides by evergreen hills, is also noted for its hiking courses, some incorporating Kamakura's well-known sights, others leading the hiker away from them.

Large, colorful maps of the city are available for ¥150 showing the location of the main shrines and temples and several hiking courses. At least one vendor recommends the Tenen Course — running along the hills to the north of the city — by virtue of the fact that it's the longest.

Alighting at Kita-Kamakura Station, set off in the direction of Kamakura. Follow the main road round to the left, crossing the tracks, until you come to Kenchoji Temple.

Kenchoji, founded in 1253, is the first of the five great Zen temples of Kamakura. In the grounds are several subtemples and buildings. The most distant of these is Hansobo, on a hill to the rear and reached via a tree-lined avenue and up a flight of steps.

Hansobo is the guardian shrine of Kenchoji and from it the Tenen Course starts off. The going is steep initially, but conditions subsequently improve. Along the way is an observation platform from which a good view of Kamakura and Sagami Bay can be obtained.

Another fine vantage point is Tendaiyama. On a clear day there is an all-round view of Kamakura, Enoshima, Mt. Fuji, Tokyo and the Boso Peninsula. Between these two observation points, on the right, is a path dropping down to secluded Kakuonji Temple.

The Tenen Course eventually descends to deposit hikers near Zuisenji Temple, founded in 1327 and featuring a Zen garden. The course is not always clear. If in doubt, remember that the path for Zuisenji bears round in the direction of Kamakura.

Another hiking course that can be picked up close to Kita-Kamakura Station is that leading to the Great Buddha. On the way, however, are many distractions.

Leaving the station, walk in the direction of Kamakura past Tokeiji Temple until coming to Jochiji Temple, to the right of the road. After exploring Jochiji, the fourth of the five great Zen temples, take the path that runs off to its left. This leads eventually to Kuzuharagaoka Park and the shrine of that name. From here it is possible to join the Great Buddha Hiking Course direct, but recommended are detours to two nearby shrines.

Walking down from Kuzuharagaoka Park, turn right into the steep hill leading down to the Zeniarai Benten Shrine. This shrine, crowded with people washing their money in the hope of seeing it increased, is approached through a tunnel.

Leaving by the rear of the shrine, head down a narrow, twisting lane toward Sasuke no Inari Shrine. The path to this shrine, which is set deep in the woods, is lined with many *torii* gates. It continues beyond the last building and rises up to join the Great Buddha Hiking Course. The course eventually comes out by a tunnel. Walk down the hill away from this tunnel, and the Great Buddha is on the left.

Another course marked on the map is the Gion San course, the start of which is a 10-minute walk from Kamakura Station. It begins to the right of Yagumo Shrine and snakes along the top of Gion Hill. There are several views of the city and Myohonji Temple. The temple is the largest Nichiren temple in Kamakura, and may be approached down a path passing by the temple cemetery.

Following the ridge of the hill along what at first appears to be a little-traveled way, hikers find the Gion San course drops sharply as it nears its conclusion. Arms, legs and backsides are necessary to ensure a safe descent. The end of the course, by the Nameir River, is not signposted but marked by perspiring figures tumbling from the undergrowth.

The latter stages of the Gion San course are not for the fashion conscious. Having said that, anything from heels to hiking boots appear the order of the day on other trails. All courses should be negotiated with care on wet days.

Hiking in Kamakura

Kamakura is easily reached from Tokyo and Yokohama by the JNR Yokosuka Line.

82

Legends and Larks in Ichikawa

Ichikawa   市川めぐり

The area around Konodai in the north of Ichikawa City, with the Edogawa River flowing nearby, was historically important as a strategic spot located between Boso to the southeast and Musashi to the west. In the 16th century it was the scene of several battles between the Satomi clan from Awa Province (in the southern part of the present Chiba Prefecture) and the Hojos from Odawara.

A particularly violent battle between the two took place in 1538, with Satomi Yoshitaka's men finally defeated by Hojo Ujitsuna's. After the defeat, a young girl appeared on the battlefield to mourn her dead father, one of the Satomis, having walked from Awa in order to do so. Completely tired out, she leaned against a stone and, it is said, cried out her father's name over and over again, weeping all the time.

She continued crying and, after a few days, passed away herself, right there on the battlefield. Every night after her death, it is said, the stone on which she had been leaning would cry, only stopping when a certain samurai appeared at the site and gave a service in honor of those who had died there.

The stone referred to in that legend, called the Yonaki (night-crying) Stone, can be found in the precincts of Soneiji Temple, adjacent to Satomi Park in Konodai. The site of this park was formerly occupied by Konodai Castle, and on one of the mounds on the river side are two stone graves of the sixth or seventh century, discovered in 1479 when Ota Dokan started building the castle.

The area was used by the military after the Meiji Restoration, and finally turned into a park in 1959. The little wooden cottage-like house in the park is the Shiensosha house, reconstructed on the spot from nearby Koiwa in 1969. It is the house where the famous poet Hakushu Kitahara (1885-1942) worked for about one year from 1916. Also located in the park are three memorial stones to the Satomis.

A short walk from Satomi Park is Junsai Pond. Walk to the far end of this — noting the "Beware of *mamushi* snakes!" signs — and turn to the right. The road leads up to an interesting little park, the Kozuka Yama Field Athletics Park, where children and adults alike can be found tackling various athletic obstacles.

Visitors to the park, which is open from 9 a.m. to 4:30 p.m. and closed on Wednesdays and rainy days, can test the Tarzan in them by "ecological running," "climbing the giraffe's neck," "climbing the elephant's leg," "passing through the whale's tummy," and so on.

Nearby the park is Ichikawa City Museum, from where a bus can be taken back to Ichikawa Station. For those not yet tired out, however, the walk is fascinating. Ichikawa is dotted with temples and shrines, and interesting architecture both new and old.

Guhoji Temple is located in a picturesque setting on a wooded hill in Mama, and is reached by climbing 63 stone steps. The precincts of the temple are extensive, but particularly notable are the black Deva King images at the entrance gate, said to have been carved by the famous sculptor Unkei (1148-1223). The temple itself was founded in the year 737.

Just below Guhoji Temple is the Tekona Reido, and another legend. Tekona was a beautiful girl who lived in Mama village and was loved by many men. At a loss as to what to do in that situation, she drowned herself, so as not to create sorrow for other people. This place of worship, founded in 1501, is dedicated to Tekona as a goddess of childbirth and child-rearing.

To reach Satomi Park, walk west from Ichikawa Station on the JNR Sobu Line, or from Konodai Station on the Keisei Line which is nearer, until you reach the Edogawa River. Then walk north along the river for about 10 minutes, and the park is just up the hill leading to the right.

Old Post-Town on Tokaido Route

Odawara 小田原

Odawara used to be an important stop on the Tokaido Highway linking Edo and Kyoto, serving as a resting place for the many travelers who would cover the distance between the two towns in some 13 days. It flourished as a post-town with many inns and tea shops, one of the 53 post-towns along the route.

The Tokaido railway line was then constructed in 1889, and from that time on the post-towns began to lose business to modern forms of transport. It now, of course, takes only three hours to travel from Tokyo to Kyoto by bullet train.

Odawara, keeping to its post-town tradition, is still firmly located on the main transport routes, but it seems to be one of those places that you're always passing through, never stopping at. Like the view of Mt. Fuji, the fleeting glimpse of Odawara Castle from the Shinkansen is as close as many people get.

The castle is, however, visited almost every day by the children who have their elementary school situated in the castle grounds, and they're no doubt glad that, unlike castles in Europe, Japanese castles, including Odawara, have no drawbridges to keep them — in this case — inside.

What they do have in this area, however, is the usual moat, which they cross every day by taking the Bridge of Study (Manabi Bashi). There are also a large number of cherry trees in this area, which make for good viewing in April.

On the way up to the main donjon is the Tokiwagi Gate, and on the other side of that, rather unexpectedly, is a small zoo. Various kinds of animals, including lions and an elephant, provide a little fun for children at the foot of the castle walls.

If the castle lacks that aged and battle-worn look which castles should have, it's not surprising. It was reconstructed as recently as 1960, for the fourth time since a structure was built there in 1495 by the Hojo family.

The original castle was apparently built on a hill in the area in about 1200. Odawara then developed as a strong regional center in the civil wars period, and under the Hojo family became the central town in the Kanto area, the castle being rebuilt as one of the largest castles in Japan.

Up the steps and into the four-storied structure, the exhibition displays weapons, swords and so on related to Odawara during the civil wars period. The fourth floor is an observation platform, from which can be seen the city of Odawara itself, the sea and island of Oshima to the south, and the hills of Hakone to the north.

The castle grounds are also famous for their plum blossom in February. Leave the Tokiwagi Gate and turn right toward the museum and library, an area with many plum trees. The museum contains various materials on the history, archaeology, plants, animals and famous figures of the Odawara region. Entrance is free, and the museum is closed on Mondays.

Not to be forgotten, of course, is your souvenir — the local *chochin* (lantern) and *kamaboko,* or steamed fishpaste cake, of which Odawara is proud. There's even a place near the station where you can see *kamaboko* being made and hear about its history. It's not to everybody's taste, but Odawara *kamaboko* is said to be the most delicious in Japan and a souvenir "must" for visitors.

Odawara can be reached by Shinkansen or Tokaido Line from Tokyo Station, or by the Odakyu Line from Shinjuku Station.

Rivers, Caves and Mountains

The Kanda River approaching Shinjuku

Every Bridge Tells a Story

Sumida River 墨田川

Times have changed since men traveled the Sumida River to visit the brothels of Yoshiwara. Now the distraction lies in the river trip itself, and the chance to shrug off Tokyo's taxis and trains and see the city from a different perspective.

"Water buses" run daily between Asakusa, the Hama Rikyu (Detached Palace) Garden and Takeshiba Pier. While the scenery along the banks is unspectacular, the pace of travel is leisurely, and the trip can be part of an outing that takes in Asakusa, the garden, and the view from the top of the nearby World Trade Center Building at Hamamatsucho.

Ten bridges span the route to Takeshiba Pier, and there is a story to each of them. Kiyosu Bridge, for example, a drawbridge, takes its name from an identical structure crossing the Rhine at Kellen, West Germany. And Kachidoki, another drawbridge, is reputedly the biggest in the Orient, but is never raised because of the heavy volume of traffic passing over it.

Komagata Bridge has a small shrine dedicated to the Bato-Kannon, an image of Kannon which has a human body with a horse's head. Umaya Bridge, another with horsey origins, is so-called after the stables that were located nearby during the Edo Period. Close to Kuramae Bridge, by the way, is the headquarters of sumo wrestling, the Kuramae Kokugikan.

As the water bus putters along with more noise than speed past the twisting and turning Shuto expressway, the river begins to open out near Hama Rikyu Garden. Directly ahead lies the expanse of Tokyo Bay, and off to the left, in the distance, the distinctive nautical outline of the Maritime Museum, and to the right, looming large, the World Trade Center Building and Tokyo Tower.

Hama Rikyu Garden is entered directly from the water bus stop. It is spacious and pleasing, and surrounded on all sides by water. A distinctive feature is the tidal pond at its center.

The garden was originally the site of a villa belonging to one of the Tokugawa shoguns, and passed into the hands of the Imperial Household in 1871. The 18th president of the United States, Ulysses S. Grant, was entertained here by the Emperor Meiji in 1879.

From Hama Rikyu Garden Hamamatsucho can be reached on foot, although it is nearer the water bus's final destination, Takeshiba Pier. From the top of the World Trade Center Building, access to which costs ¥400, it is possible to look back along the route just taken. Hama Rikyu Garden is spread out clearly below and there are also fine views of downtown Tokyo and Tokyo Bay.

The *suijo bus* on the Sumida River

The *Suijo Bus* (water bus) terminal at Asakusa is very close to Asakusa Station on the Ginza subway line, by Azuma Bridge. A one-way trip costs adults ¥400 and children ¥240.

That Old Man River...

Kanda River 神田川

In the midst of the strolling young couples, joggers and musicians of Inokashira Park are others who giggle and splash across the waters of Inokashira Lake. In hired boats they row to where the lake ends by a small stone gate and miniature bridge, and then head back. The water, however, keeps on going. It flows on for another 25 km, under 130-odd bridges and through eight districts until it reaches the Sumida River on the other side of the city.

This is the Kanda River, the at times drab and often overlooked urban waterway that threads its way across Tokyo and helps to draw some of its boundaries on the way.

For much of the time the concrete-banked Kanda resembles a canal with the plug pulled out, but its origins are natural. Beginning in Inokashira Park in Mitaka district, it runs through Suginami, Shinjuku, Nakano, Bunkyo, Chiyoda and Taito wards before reaching the Sumida River in Chuo Ward, just past Yanagi Bridge, the last of the many that span it.

The Kanda was formerly split into three. From Inokashira Park to Otaki Bridge in Bunkyo Ward, it was known as the Kanda Josui (aqueduct); from Otaki Bridge to Funakawara Bridge by Iidabashi as the Edogawa River (hence the existence of Edogawa Bridge), not to be confused with the Edogawa River in Edogawa Ward; and from Funakawara Bridge to the Sumida River as the Kanda River.

Not until 1965 did the entire length become known as the Kanda River, when waterways around the country were reclassified. Nevertheless, it is the originally named Kanda River, broader and deeper than the rest, which most resembles a major waterway, as this stretch was once widened by the Sendai *daimyo* on the orders of the Tokugawa shogunate to make it more accessible to traffic.

The Kanda flows from east to west. To its north, across the Chuo Line, another river begins at Zenpukuji Park. The Zenpukuji River passes under the railway tracks near Ogikubo and the gap between it and the Kanda narrows until the two meet with little ceremony under a power cable near Nakano Fujimicho Station on the Marunouchi subway line.

Still a third river, north of the Zenpukuji, drops down to join the Kanda at Shimo Ochiai. This is the Myoshoji River, which leaves Myoshoji Park in Suginami Ward on its journey downtown.

A trip along the banks of the Kanda River is no stroll, as no continuous walking course exists from end to end. On leaving Inokashira Park the river passes through an idyllic landscape of meadow and trees before slipping between spanking new concrete banks at Mitakadai Station. The first bridge past the station, to quell any doubts, is the Kanda Bridge.

The river passes by mile after mile of Tokyo mediocrity: two-story apartment buildings that look older than their years; overhead expressways and small playgrounds; baseball diamonds and vending machines; railway lines and narrow lanes.

As the Kanda moves deeper into Tokyo, more and more businesses spring up in the backstreets around its banks: not just *sake* shops and greengrocers, but tailors and *futon* makers, printers and mechanics. In the smallest alley there is commercial activity.

There are also some interesting perspectives, such as the familiar Shinjuku skyline rising at the head of the river, which really seems about to flow into the lobby of the Century Hyatt Hotel before it veers sharply to the north to pass back under the Chuo Line by Higashi Nakano Station.

Past Higashi Nakano the river is attractively banked. It leads on to Ochiai Park, a recreational area ingeniously built atop a sewage works. Somewhere in the vicinity a pipe has access to the river. Conservationists take note: from it detergent pours, turning Kanda into a sudsy channel and tainting the air around. Further back, signs were beseeching, "Let's clean up the Kanda!" — but they didn't mean with soap.

Demarcating the border of Shinjuku and Bunkyo wards, the river runs for a short time in parallel with Tokyo's only surviving tram line, linking Minowa, north of Asakusa, and Waseda.

Nearby the Waseda terminus is Shin Edogawa Park, a pleasant Japanese garden that rises up in a wooded hill.

Beyond Edogawa Bridge and the subway stop of the same name, the river flows under an elevated expressway until Suidobashi. Beyond, the ground rises, affording one of the better-known views of the Kanda River, looking down from Ochanomizu Bridge.

Then it's on to the Sumida, where the bridges are bigger, the boats more numerous — and Inokashira Park seems a long way away.

Shooting the Rapids at Nagatoro

Nagatoro 長瀞

The narrow road lined with souvenir shops and restaurants leads quickly down from the station to the river, but at first sight, disappointment reigns. The color of the water is a creamy brown, not the glistening blue which you see in guidebook photographs, and Nagatoro seems to be just one more tourist hoax.

Retreating back up the road, a small second-floor coffee shop offers the chance to put a brake on flagging spirits. "It was much cleaner five years ago," says the owner, "but the dam and other construction work seem to have soiled it up."

It doesn't seem to have stopped tourists from coming, however, and soon you're back down among them on the banks of perhaps Chichibu's most popular sightseeing spot, in the northwest of Saitama Prefecture. Nagatoro extends along the Ara River for 6 km altogether, between Takasagobashi Bridge and Oyahanabashi Bridge.

What makes it famous is the gorge located midway between these bridges and starting where the road from the station ends, a one-kilometer-long embankment of crystalline schist rock jutting out here and there in various unusual formations.

A walk along the rocks leads you toward Oyahanabashi Bridge, to the point where the river branches into two rapid stretches — a popular place for canoeists and for those who just like to dangle their feet in the cool water. From the other direction come the Japanese-style boats carrying their cargoes of tourists over the rapids. These boats "shooting the rapids" ply between the two bridges from March to November, stopping off near Nagatoro Station, and offer good views of the rocky cliffs. The area is especially picturesque in spring and autumn.

The history of the boats goes back to the time when Nagatoro (then Hodosan) Station was opened in 1911, for tourist purposes. After that, a festival was held to pray for safety and to express gratitude to the god of water, and although its origins are not clearly known, this developed into the festival of fire and water known as the Funadama Festival, held every year on Aug. 15. A wonderful atmosphere is achieved in the evening, people sitting atop the rocks watching dedicatory lanterns being floated on the river from lantern-bedecked boats under an umbrella of fantastic fireworks.

For those who want to know more about the rocks, Chichibu Natural History Museum is located nearby, and the other spot to visit is Hodosan Shrine and Mount Hodo, only 497 meters high but offering nice views of the surrounding Chichibu area. A ropeway hoists people up the mountain, and a horse-drawn tourist carriage goes from the station to the shrine, although anyone with a heart, on seeing the horses plodding wearily along, will walk themselves. Hodosan Shrine festival is held annually on April 3.

Bicycles are available for rent from several places near the station, and it won't be long before you forget about the color of the water. For those who wish to extend their stay, the SL Hotel offers unique accommodation in railway carriages. For information, call 04946-6-3011.

To reach Nagatoro, take the Seibu Ikebukuro superexpress to Chichibu (just over an hour), then change to the local Chichibu Line for Nagatoro (25 minutes).

Dwellings, Graves, or What?

Yoshimi Caves 吉見百穴

The Yoshimi caves in Saitama have puzzled people ever since investigations of them began in 1887. It had been known that a cluster of holes existed on the small hill even before then, and that is probably how they got their Japanese name of Yoshimi Hyakuketsu. However, proper excavations began in the Meiji Period, the impetus coming partly from a visit to the caves by Edward Morse.

Morse (1838-1925) was an American who did much to stimulate interest in archaeology in Japan. It was he who excavated the Omori shell mound in 1877, a project said to have been the first such scientific excavation to take place in Japan.

Morse visited the Yoshimi caves in 1882, and his interpretation was that they were Korean graves, while other people thought they were ancient dwellings of some sort. Research beginning in 1887 discovered over 200 holes and various implements, as well as human bones.

One theory at the time held that they were the dwellings of *tsuchigumo,* a tribe of cavedwellers thought to have inhabited ancient Japan, but gradually research progressed and by the 1920s it was back to the grave theory. However, even then the story was only just beginning, for further analysis of the caves revealed new details.

For example, as can be seen from an exploration of them, all the holes have a similar structure of an inner room and a narrow passageway leading to it. Most inner rooms have a raised platform, presumably for coffins, but some have none at all. Moreover, the shapes of the rooms and passages were found to vary, with eight types of inner room identified. Most of them are square, very few round.

Unfortunately, investigations came to an abrupt end with the war, and a large cave was built in the hill as an underground plant, with the result that some caves were lost. After the war, local residents started a preservation society, and investigations revealed a total of 219 caves remaining.

Next came the problem of the distribution of the caves. As can be seen, they get larger the higher up the hill you go, and there seems to be greater space between the holes at the top of the hill. Also, research has revealed that some relation might exist between the position of the passageway and that of the coffin inside the room.

Nobody has yet come up with full explanations to all the problems, but the guide book on sale at the caves suggests that they were family graves of the Late Tumulus Period, about 1,300 years ago. People at that time, it says, considered death to be the start of a long journey to the next world, where life was the same as in the present one.

Hence perhaps the symbolic passage leading to the inner room, while the room itself probably followed the shape of the dwelling the family lived in. Similarly, the family grave theory might explain the different sizes of the rooms, rather than status, period and so on.

Research has come a long way from theories of *tsuchigumo*, now known to have been a legendary tribe, but the continuing mysteries make a visit all the more intriguing. Similar caves have been found in other areas of soft rock, but the Yoshimi caves are the biggest cluster.

The Yoshimi caves are located 10 minutes by Tobu bus (for Konosu) from Higashi Matsuyama on the Tobu Tojo Line from Ikebukuro.

Underground Buddhist Sculptures

Taya Caves   田谷の洞窟

Ofuna has long existed in the shadow of its famous neighbor, Kamakura, despite the fact that it possesses a number of equally interesting attractions. The flower center used to be considered only as an extension of a visit to Kamakura, but now Ofuna is worthy of a visit by itself, and it has the symbol to prove it.

The white image of Kannon, the goddess of mercy, shines a welcome and indeed one of the best views of the statue can be had from the approaching train. It is located on a steep, low hill just to the west of the station, some five minutes' climb after crossing the river.

The history of the statue is not as imposing as the sight itself. Planned at the beginning of the Showa Period and dedicated, it is said, to peace and the improvement of social conditions, work began on it in 1929, and although the basic contour was completed, work was halted as a result of the war. The Goddess was left out in the cold as a rough concrete image for almost 20 years before being finally completed in 1960.

Ofuna's symbol may be relatively new, but the history of the area runs deep. From the bus terminal at the foot of the Kannon hill, a bus for Yokohama Dreamland stops at Taya, about an eight-minute ride. A short walk from the bus stop leads to Josenji Temple, an unobtrusive structure sheltering the Taya Caves, located just to the right of the temple. Entrance to the caves costs ¥300, in exchange for which you receive a small candle and information sheet which tells you that the caves were dug out of the sandstone rock by hand.

The process began in the 12th century, when the caves were possibly used for storing weapons and treasure, although it has also been suggested that the caves existed to an extent many years even before that, possibly as dwellings. What is certain, however, is that by the middle ages the caves were being used for religious purposes by members of the Shingon sect of Buddhism. The caves were gradually extended for this purpose and have a total length of 1.5 km, about 400 meters of which are now open to the public.

Crouching down into the narrow entrance, you are led away by the darkness and sound of trickling water and a splendid network of tunnels is revealed, passing on from one dome-shaped compartment to another. These were exercise places for members of the sect and there are 17 in all. Each compartment bears sculptures of Buddhism, presumably carved by members of the sect while doing underground training. The disciples would sit in the exercise halls for 21-day fasts, meditating and digging the cliff by hand.

The caves are actually three stories high and the tunnels wind their way around the hill into a complex network including ventilation tunnels and a drainage system. With buildings going up and up in the cities, it is a good feeling to go down into the caves, although visitors are requested to respect them and refrain from adding their own designs to the walls.

The caves were closed during the anti-Buddhist movement of the Meiji Period but survived the threat and were reopened again in 1927. The light at the end of the tunnel brings you back to Josenji Temple, which was built in 1532 to protect the caves.

Ofuna is located one hour from Shinagawa by the Keihin Tohoku, Tokaido or Yokosuka lines.

Plenty of Fresh Air and Nature

Mt. Takao 高尾山

Cheaply and easily reached from Tokyo, Mount Takao is the place to go for fresh air, beautiful scenery and plenty of exercise. With time at a premium for most people, the thickly wooded slopes have been mapped out almost to a fault to help hikers make the most of their day out. There are no less than six different walking courses to choose from, four of which lead to the 600-meter-high summit.

All have a theme embracing nature, and judging from the crowds, Course No. 1 — labeled simply "Nature" — is the most popular. This follows the original mountain path to Yakuo-in Temple, said to have been founded in 744, then continues to the summit. Mostly paved and much patronized, this route is a hikers' equivalent of the busy Chuo Expressway visible far below.

Course No. 1 can be walked from the base of Mount Takao or joined halfway after an ascent in either a cable car or chair lift. From the cable car terminus two alternative, and in many ways more "natural," routes to the top are only a brief walk away, as is a short looped course through surrounding forest. One of these, Course 4, passes across a suspension bridge.

To the southwest of the summit, which grows very crowded around lunchtime, stands Mount Fuji. To the east lies the Kanto Plain, and working round, Tokyo and Sagami bays. On an exceptionally clear day — just after a typhoon, for example — there are some truly spectacular views to be had from Mount Takao, particularly of Tokyo, but more usually the capital is shrouded in haze.

From the top it is possible to continue on for several kilometers to Lake Sagami, or mountain-hop round to Hachioji. These trails are well signposted.

A recommended descent is by Course 6 — "Forest and Water" — which follows a mountain stream and passes by a waterfall before emerging a 10-minute walk from Takaosan-guchi cable car and chair lift terminus and the Takao Museum of Natural History.

Halfway back up Takao, near the other end of the cable car line, is the Takao Natural Park. The monkeys and deer are the main attractions here. Visitors enter a large enclosure and stand among the only species of monkey native to Japan. A keeper gives a short talk and answers any questions that arise.

Early starters for Mt. Takao should make breakfast a bowl of *tororo soba*. Thickened with grated mountain yam, this soba, for which Mount Takao is noted, is an ideal way to begin a hike.

A scene of the *hiwatari* festival on Mt. Takao (see Calendar)

Takaosan-guchi Station is reached from Shinjuku Station on the Keio Line in 43 minutes by express on Sundays and holidays, and 54 minutes on weekdays. The cost one way is ¥280. If going by JNR, take the Chuo Line to Takao Station and then change to the Keio Line for the short ride to Takaosan-guchi.

Something Everyone Does Once

Mt. Fuji   富士山

The idea of scaling Mount Fuji is an irresistible one for most people, although they may wish they had known better after actually realizing their dream. Nevertheless, for those who must try everything at least once, the following is a short guide on how to ascend — and descend from — Japan's most famous peak.

The official mountain-climbing season opens on July 1 and lasts for two months. There are four paths leading to the top. They start, respectively, from Kawaguchiko, Fujinomiya, Gotenba and Subashiri. As a rule, climbers ascend by means of either of the former two routes and descend along either of the latter two.

The first route is from Kawaguchiko Station in Yamanashi Prefecture. The Kawaguchi express train directly links Kawaguchiko Station with Shinjuku Station in Tokyo (a two-hour trip), and many extra trains are scheduled during the climbing season.

In front of Kawaguchiko Station, a bus runs from stop No. 7, taking climbers directly to the fifth (Kawaguchiko) station in one hour.

An alternative is the bus that runs from the west exit of JNR's Shinjuku or Hamamatsucho stations. The bus takes climbers directly to the fifth station in two hours and 25 minutes. From there, climbers must walk. It takes five hours to reach the peak. Reservations may be made by telephone; the number is 03-374-2221.

The second route is from Fujinomiya Station in Shizuoka Prefecture, which is linked with Fuji Station on the Minobe Line (20 minutes). A bus runs from the front of Fujinomiya Station to the fifth Fujinomiya station.

Another means of getting there is from Mishima Station on the Shinkansen line in Shizuoka Prefecture. Climbers can take a bus from the No. 2 bus stop in front of the south exit of the station (a two-hour, five-minute trip).

Most people use the third, Gotenba route to descend from the peak, this taking about two hours and 40 minutes to accomplish. From the fifth station, a bus takes climbers to Gotenba Station (45 minutes) from which an express train can be taken for the trip back to Tokyo Station.

The fourth route permits a quick (two-hour) descent from the peak to the Subashiri fifth station. A bus from the station takes climbers directly to Subashiri Shrine in about 45 minutes, where buses leave for Gotenba Station (20 minutes) and Fujiyoshida Station (40 minutes).

Mt. Fuji

Seashores and Islands

Enoshima

Satellite of Surf and Sand

Fujisawa 藤沢

The city of Fujisawa is a blend of suburbia and resort. A residential satellite of Tokyo daily disgorging commuters bound for the big city, it also attracts flocks of day-trippers headed for the beaches that lie to its south.

The focal point of leisure activity is the wooded island of Enoshima which lies just offshore and is joined to the mainland by Benten Bridge. On either side of the bridge, beaches spread out — to the east in the direction of Kamakura, to the west following the curve of the coast round to Chigasaki and beyond.

Just down coastal Route 134 heading toward Chigasaki are an aquarium (on the right) and Enoshima Marineland and Enoshima Zoo (both on the left). Enoshima Marineland and the zoo have regular shows starring various sea animals, including seals, porpoises and penguins. Admission is charged.

Between the beach and the main road — which is lined with hotels and chain restaurants and wouldn't look out of place in a U.S. resort — is an 8.4-km cycling course providing a constant view of the ocean. Bicycles can be hired free of charge for three hours at the Enoshima end of the course. The bicycle office is about a 20-minute walk from Benten Bridge, past the aquarium, marineland and zoo.

In the summer months the beaches are heavily patronized, particularly around Enoshima, where refreshments, sunshades and deckchairs are available, but throughout the year, the coastline is the preserve of surfers and windsurfers.

For those interested in surfing (though be warned, the waves aren't very big) but lack equipment, boards are available for hire at surf shops in the area. Surf and Sands (Tel. 0467-33-3690) rents out boards for ¥3,000 per two hours and ¥5,000 for the whole day. The shop is just off the coast road on Masagodori Avenue, which is accessible by bus from Tsujido Station of the JNR. Goddess International (Tel. 0467-86-8131) has boards available for ¥1,000 per two hours, or ¥3,000 for the whole day. The store is on Route 134, a 15-minute walk from JNR Chigasaki Station.

Goddess International also runs, year round, a windsurfing school at weekends. A day's instruction, board and wetsuit provided, costs ¥5,000. It is necessary to make reservations ahead of time.

The crowded beach scenes in mid-summer are raw material for stories about overcrowding in Japan. For those used to desert islands, it might come as a bit of a shock. But the sight of Mt. Fuji far down the coast — when it's visible — is fair compensation.

The JNR Tokaido Main Line runs through Chigasaki, Tsujido and Fujisawa. Alternatively, the Odakyu Line from Shinjuku runs via Fujisawa to Katase-Enoshima Station. A small electric railway, the Enoden, links Fujisawa and Kamakura, and includes stops at Enoshima and Shonan Kaigan Koen from where the coast is a short walk.

'The Way to Fish Paradise'

Aburatsubo   油壺

Many small bays and inlets make up the southwestern shoreline of the Miura Peninsula, which juts out between Tokyo and Sagami bays and forms with the Boso Peninsula the Uraga Straits.

One popular destination is Aburatsubo, which literally means "oil pot," drawing its name, it is said, from the oily-calm waters that rub against its shores. Aburatsubo boasts a well-stocked yachting marina, a few research buildings belonging to Tokyo University and the Aburatsubo Marine Park.

The marine park bears all the hallmarks of a "tourist spot," having its quota of noisy game centers, mechanical rides, a ubiquitous public address system and a souvenir shop built into the exit.

The unimaginative architecture does its best to put a damper on nature's charms, but once inside the aquarium, all is forgotten on a stroll down "The Way to Fish Paradise." The display of marine life lining this route to the heaven of the deep is nothing if not thorough, covering everything from freshwater fish to the four-eyed, the land-walking to the upside down.

There are 30 numbered display tanks on the first floor whose inhabitants are variously darting, delightful, bloated or bizarre. Some, the goatfish and ponyfish, for example, are named after creatures of the dry land, but the resemblance is not always apparent. Others are more romantically dubbed rose fish and sweet lip, while there is nothing romantic about the slippery dick or banded humbug, but at least it's easy to see how they earned their names.

The second floor features a large circular tank in which fish of all sizes whirl round and round. For people watching, it's like being in the middle of a marine merry-go-round. A diver enters the tank to feed fish by hand at certain times during the day.

From Aburatsubo a ferry runs to the island of Jogashima, lying just off the tip of the peninsula and serving as a breakwater for the fishing port of Misaki. Alternatively, Jogashima can be reached by bus across a 575-meter-long toll bridge.

There are a lighthouse and lighthouse museum on the island, both atop an untidy-looking hill. The view, however, is rather more appealing, and there are plenty of interesting rocks to scramble over further down.

Other unusual cliffs, shaped by the action of the waves, can be found further back up the Miura Peninsula at Arasaki, and a walk along the seashore at Akiya turns up numerous pieces of bottle glass, smoothed and rounded by the action of salt water.

The Miura Peninsula is accessible from Tokyo via the Yokosuka Line, which passes through Kamakura, Zushi and Yokosuka before reaching its Kurihama terminus. Buses run from Zushi, Yokosuka and Kurihama to the port of Misaki, from which Jogashima and Aburatsubo are easily reached.

Across the Benten Bridge

Enoshima 江の島

Legend has it that Enoshima just happened to pop up out of the sea one moment in the distant past, nobody can say exactly when. The long sandbank connecting the small island to the mainland suggests the more plausible story, that the power of the sea gradually ate away the hook of land until the island broke away. Now Enoshima is found floating off the shore near Kamakura and provides the visitor with an excellent small-scale hiking course.

Entry to the island is gained by walking the Benten Bridge over the lapping sea. There is a parallel bridge for traffic next to the pedestrian crossing. From the end of the bridge, through the *torii* gate, a steep, narrow road leads up into the hill toward Enoshima Shrine. The road is lined with inns and souvenir shops as it must have been in the Edo Period, when Enoshima first began to attract visitors from Edo on a large scale.

Enoshima Shrine is in fact the name given to three shrines on the island, Hetsunomiya, Nakatsunomiya and Okutsunomiya. The original Enoshima Shrine is said to have been located in the sea-eroded caves on the southern side of the island and it was in the caves that the famous Hadaka (Naked) Benten rested. The beautiful statue, which later became a symbol for Kabuki actors and entertainers, is now situated in the grounds of Hetsunomiya Shrine, together with an image of Happi Benten.

Since 1959, the shrines have been connected by an escalator, but the walk is more rewarding. The busiest of the three, Hetsunomiya Shrine, built in 1206 and rebuilt in 1976, is approached by an ascent of some 300 steps, and the climb then leads on to Nakatsunomiya Shrine.

The path continues from Nakatsunomiya to Enoshima Tropical Garden, the terminal point of the escalator. This tropical garden, perched on the very roof of Enoshima, was previously used by priests of the temple as land for growing vegetables.

Also situated in the tropical garden is the peace tower, a dizzy climb up the twisting stairs of which reveals a view of the garden below, the island itself, the "Miami of the East" coastline nearby and, in the distance, Oshima Island and Mt. Fuji. On top of the tower is a lighthouse, first operated in 1951. The tower itself rises 53.7 meters from the ground and 113 meters above sea level.

The steps leading down from the tropical garden (entrance ¥200) lead past numerous small shops and eating places to the stone *torii* of the Okutsunomiya Shrine. This arch was dedicated to the shrine in 1182 by Minamoto Yoritomo, founder of the Kamakura shogunate, and lends a historical atmosphere to the entrance to the quietest of the shrines.

From here the sea beckons and the path bends down to a rocky area called Chigogafuchi, a kind of veranda looking out to sea. It used to be possible to follow the path into the Benten caves, but they have been closed since 1970 because of the danger from falling rocks.

At a cost of ¥200, a boat will ferry you around the island from this spot, past the Shonanko Lighthouse on the east side of the island to the yacht harbor, completed in 1964 and the busy site of the yacht events of the Tokyo Olympics.

Enoshima is reached from Shinjuku by the Odakyu Line (Katase-Enoshima Station), or by the Yokosuka Line from Shinagawa to Ofuna, changing onto the monorail which swings you to Enoshima in 13 minutes.

Tokyo's Tropical Paradise

Ogasawara Islands 小笠原

Metropolitan Tokyo doesn't stop at the grey waters of Tokyo Bay. For administrative purposes it skips down the seven islands of the Izu chain, and then leaps on from the last of these, Hachijojima, to the unspoilt beaches, palm trees and turquoise bays of the Ogasawara Islands.

Lying 1,000 km to the southeast of Tokyo, the Ogasawara (or Bonin) Islands — only two of which are inhabited — have no airport, one television station and a population that could fit aboard a Yamanote Line train.

The 3,500-ton Ogasawara Maru links Tokyo's Takeshiba Sanbashi Pier with the main island of Chichijima in 28-1/2 hours. The blue-and-white vessel ferries across not only islanders, holidaymakers and workmen but also newspapers, mail, provisions and the taped news and shows that make up Chichijima's few hours of nightly television fare.

As the Ogasawara Maru enters Chichijima's Futami Harbor, two long blasts of its horn draw to the waterfront dockworkers, sightseers, policemen and innkeepers, the latter bringing large signs to woo tourists as they step down the gangway.

This is nothing compared to the send-off, however, when several hundred people gather to bid an island farewell. To cheers and shouts, and to the strains of Auld Lang Syne, many passengers embark with boxes of papaya under their arms and leis of hibiscus around their necks. A flotilla of small boats escorts the Tokyo-bound ship across harbor, a bugle sounds and the Ogasawara Maru sails away leaving a train of bright red flowers in its wake.

Said to have been discovered by Sadayori Ogasawara in 1592, the islands were subsequently claimed for England and King George by a Captain Beechey in 1827, visited by Commodore Perry 26 years later and eventually turned over to Japan in 1875. During World War II the civilian population was evacuated and the Imperial Japanese Army moved in. With Japan's defeat, the U.S. Navy took control, and remained a presence until June 26, 1968, when the islands came under the jurisdiction of Metropolitan Tokyo.

It was in 1830 (also on June 26) that the first party of settlers — a handful of Americans, Europeans and Hawaiians — arrived from the Sandwich Islands (now Hawaii) and made Chichijima their home.

It is worth making a trip to the cemetery on the hill behind Chichijima's Maritime Self-Defense Force base to appreciate something of the island's history. Here are tombstones to the memory of Gilley, Gonzales, Washington and Savory. "Sacred to the memory of Nathanial Savory," reads one, "a native of Bradford in Essex County, Mass., U.S.A. and one of the first settlers of this island who departed this life April 10, 1874. Aged 80 years."

From the more recent past, traces of wartime endeavor remain. Although Chichijima was never invaded, Japanese forces prepared for the worst. One estimate puts the number of tunnels dug on the island at almost 340. Walk into the hills and sooner or later a pillbox, concrete bunker or gloomy passage looms from the undergrowth.

In the bay is the wreck of a freighter, as popular among tourists as St. George's Church, the present structure a gift of the U.S. Navy "to the military and civilian populace of the Bonin Volcano Islands."

Jungle trails abound on both Chichijima and neighboring Hahajima. Sufficiently well signposted that the hiker never quite gets lost, the foliage is at times dense enough to make him think he might. Unlike Okinawa, which lies on the same latitude and has poisonous snakes, there are no dangerous animals abroad on the Ogasawara Islands — just birds, bats, goats and the Giant African Snail, not a danger but a pest.

But if there are no snakes or worse on dry land, sand tiger sharks

111

occasionally come up to shore to bask in the sun-streamed shallows. Many beautiful fish reward the diver's efforts, the islands play host to turtles, and sometimes it is possible to catch sight of a whale on the 2-1/2-hour journey between Chichijima and Hahajima.

Not everyone will have time to visit Hahajima, population a little over 300 and 54 km distant from Chichijima. The island is long and beautiful, and truly represents a chance to "get away from it all." Accommodation on Hahajima is limited, so it is necessary to make reservations in advance. Also, be sure to check the schedule of the Hahajima Maru, as it doesn't sail daily.

Fishing is a popular pastime on the Ogasawara Islands — and an experience from the side of an outrigger canoe. The water is so clear that anglers can watch their prey decide whether or not to bite. As for swimming, there are many opportunities. Sharks notwithstanding, conditions off these coral strewn shores are some of the best.

A descendant of Nathanial Savory laments the changes that have taken place since his great grandfather's day — the disappearance of big trees and the building up of the harbor. "These must have been beautiful islands when my great grandfather first came here. Paradise," he sighs. By most people's standards, they still are.

Ogasawara—Tokyo's tropical islands

Fairs and Markets

Tsukiji Wholesale Market

Good for Picking Up a Bargain

Antique Fairs   新井薬師／乃木神社

There is something antique-like about temples and shrines, and there is something reverend about antiques. So it seems quite natural that if you are going to hold an antique fair, an excellent place to do so would be in the grounds of such a place.

Araiyakushi Temple in Nakano Ward is the site of an antique fair on the first Sunday of every month. The dealers, who come from as far away as Hokkaido and as near as Nakano Broadway, set up their wares as the sun rises, and put what's left away when the sun sets, weather, of course, permitting.

Some 60 dealers take part, offering a variety of wares ranging from elegant pottery to battered old type-writers, from proud grandfather-like clocks to old picture postcards. Prices are rather expensive, but simply to go and have a look around can be a pleasure in itself.

The antiques, spread out on the ground, fit well into the background and atmosphere which the temple provides, especially as it has a reputation for being a lively, bustling place. Local fairs are still held on the 8th, 18th and 28th of each month, but the story really goes back to the Edo Period. At that time it was said that a medicine sold at the temple was a cure for all kinds of children's illnesses. The place was always busy with people going to the temple to either buy the cure or offer thanks for the recovery which magically appeared.

The legend has since changed owing to an event in 1629 when a daughter of Tokugawa Hidetada, suffering from an eye illness which all other medicines failed to cure, visited the temple and prayed. The prayers were answered and legend now connects

114

Araiyakushi Temple with the healing of eye diseases.

On the second Sunday of each month a flea market is held at **Nogi Shrine** in Akasaka, set in Nogizaka Park and dedicated to Gen. Maresuke Nogi who lived here around the turn of the century. His mansion still stands in its own garden to the left of the entrance to the shrine.

Gen. Nogi was born in 1849 and, after a rigorous military education, had a distinguished military career which included twice capturing Port Arthur. He became a national hero after the victory against Russia in 1905, his popularity enhanced by his modest character and apparent lack of ambition.

Nogi was looked upon as a model of disciplined loyalty to the Meiji throne, to his country and to the military values which he was educated in. Upon the death of the emperor in September 1912, Nogi committed *hara-kiri,* an act of self-sacrifice and loyalty which led to the dedication of this shrine. His wife Shizuko committed suicide with him.

Local fairs are held at Nogi Shrine every month on the 1st and 13th, and every year Sept. 13, being the day of Nogi's death, is marked by a festival. Other antique markets are held on the first floor of Sunshine City in Ikebukuro on the third Saturday and Sunday of each month; on the steps of the Roi Building in Roppongi on the fourth Thursday and Friday (Tel. 03-404-2357); and at Togo Shrine in Shibuya Ward on the fourth Sunday (Tel. 03-403-3591).

Araiyakushi Temple is located a short walk from Araiyakushimae Station on the Seibu Shinjuku Line. Tel. 03-386-1355.

Nogi Shrine is easily reached from Nogizaka Station on the Chiyoda subway line. Tel. 03-402-2181.

Colorful Slice of Japanese Life

Tsukiji Fish Market   築地場外市場

For those who wish to experience a colorful slice of Japanese life that is not an annual festival but business as usual for thousands, a visit to the Tokyo central wholesale market at Tsukiji is a must.

Founded in 1935 by the metropolitan government, the central wholesale market originally consisted of three regional markets at Tsukiji, Kanda and Koto, but with the increase in population and improvement in living standards the number of regional and branch markets has since jumped.

Bounded on two sides by Hama Rikyu Garden and the Sumida River, and with its main entrance facing the Asahi Shimbun building, Tsukiji handles both marine products and fruit and vegetables, with an emphasis on its role as a fish market.

While much of the catch is domestic, fish is also imported. That put on sale fresh is flown into Japan, the rest arriving frozen or salted.

A major imported species such as shrimp, for example, comes from all over the world. *Uni* (sea urchin) is flown in from Los Angeles and Vancouver, and other *sushi* shop favorites such as squid and tuna likewise come from abroad. *Tai* (sea bream), an essential at the Japanese wedding table, is mostly imported.

On the domestic side it is not uncommon for fish to be trucked in live from Hokkaido in special air tanks, or driven fresh to market as soon as it has been landed. The price differential for live, very fresh and older fish is tremendous.

Tsukiji has undergone considerable changes since 1935. It was built to be supplied by ship and rail, and now is fed almost entirely by truck. Hence the bumper-to-bumper traffic that can be seen any morning as 17,000 trucks roll by. Vehicles apart, it is estimated that 70,000 people go in and out of Tsukiji daily.

Tsukiji has also been affected by changes in the distribution system in Japan, with more and more of the total volume of retail purchasing being done through supermarkets. Although some of the smaller chains do their purchasing at Tsukiji, the larger supermarkets like Seibu and Ito-Yokado do much of it outside, sidestepping not only the central wholesale market but trading companies as well. A great deal of the market's business today is therefore providing fresh fish for *sushi* shops and restaurants.

To see the market in action, it is best to go early. Goods up for sale at a morning auction start coming in from the afternoon of the day before, and are displayed by category in their assigned place at the market overnight. These are goods brought from the producers by Tsukiji's wholesalers. Before auctioning begins — at 5:40 a.m. for fish and 6:20 a.m. for fruit and vegetables — buyers, who wear caps for ease of identification, can be seen inspecting the day's lots. This is called *shitami* (preliminary inspection).

When auctioning begins, the auctioneers, who sit on a dais, call out prices and the buyers bid with hands and *teyari* (fingers). The bidders are both authorized buyers — large consumers, retailers, food processors and private market wholesalers — and middlemen, of whom there are about 1,300 at Tsukiji, who between the hours of 7 a.m. and 11 a.m. sell to smaller retailers and restaurant operators what they have purchased at auction.

Walking up and down between their stalls is perhaps Tsukiji's most rewarding experience, but not without danger as knives and hooks flash, electric saws bite into frozen tuna, heavily laden trolleys career round tight corners at a moment's notice and buyers push by brusquely in a hurry to be done.

In places the floor is cobbled, overhead the roof is a great, ramshackle corrugated iron affair, outside little-used railway tracks grow rusty, and within, bare electric light bulbs illuminate the staggering variety of produce on display.

Japanese food, they say, is designed to appeal as much to the eye as to the palate, and a visit to Tsukiji shows this holds true all the way from the marketplace to the plate. It is worth having a look at the produce laid out for the buyers to inspect before auctioning begins to see just how carefully it has been arranged, and then to see how equally carefully the middlemen stock their stalls afterward.

Walking out from the center of the market, past buckets of eels, men at work with mallet and iron wedge, over rubbish and through a gap in the stream of porters and their trolleys, one reaches the outer fringes of Tsukiji where shops sell everything from Wellington boots — standard footwear for market workers — to plastic *bento* trays and other catering necessities. In addition, there are numerous cheap eateries to feed the hungry, as early morning work is guaranteed to build up an appetite.

The market is open every day except Sundays, national holidays and the year-end and New Year periods.

To reach Tsukiji, and to reach it at its most interesting, rise very early — don't worry, you're not the only one — and take the subway to Tsukiji Station on the Hibiya subway line, then follow the Wellington boots. Tsukiji is also accessible from the Shinbashi Station of the JNR and Ginza subway line.

Museums and Archives

Kite Museum

Bringing Traditional Music Alive

Michio Miyagi Memorial Hall   宮城道雄記念館

Michio Miyagi was born in Kobe in 1894. At the age of one he contracted an eye disease and by 7 he was totally blind. For a blind person at that time, the choice of future career was simple: masseur or musician. Miyagi's parents decided on the latter and sent their son off to a local *koto* teacher.

That was the tragic start to what became a brilliant musical career. By the age of 11, Miyagi had got the fourth and highest degrees in both *koto* and *shamisen*. At 13 the family went to Korea, where Miyagi's father was seriously disabled, leaving Michio as the breadwinner. He supported his family by teaching the *koto* and *shamisen*, and also at this time started composing, his first piece being "The Transformations of Water."

On returning to Japan, Miyagi moved to Tokyo and continued his career as teacher, composer and writer until his tragic death in 1956. Such was his influence on the Japanese music world that in 1978 a museum dedicated to his life and career was opened in Shinjuku Ward's Nakamachi, on the site where Miyagi spent his later years.

The Michio Miyagi Memorial Hall is said to be the first museum in Japan to be dedicated to a musician. Up the steps of the Western-style main building and through the glass doors, the reception room offers books, records and tapes for sale, and various information sheets about the museum. Very conveniently, there is an English-language tape guide available for English-speaking visitors which gives a detailed explanation of the main display hall.

From the reception room, you enter the foyer and to the right behind you is the main hall. In the entrance is a bust of Miyagi, and

120

the 13-stringed *koto* which he played in his later years. Listening to the tape, we hear that "Miyagi was the first modern composer to breathe new vitality into traditional Japanese music, in particular introducing elements of Western music."

Among the instruments on display is the 17-string *koto* which Miyagi invented to make bass notes easier. Miyagi pioneered many new developments, such as the use of the left hand in playing the *koto,* and was a leader of the New Japanese Music Movement of the 1920s.

Across the foyer is the listening room, with a video program which changes with the seasons and stereo booths with headphones for private listening to a selection of tapes. In the main hall, also, there is a video of Miyagi performing, and there are three earphone guides in the corners giving explanations in Japanese and pieces of music, so that the visitor can enjoy listening in the museum as well as just looking.

Behind the main building is the study which Miyagi used after 1948, and a recording studio which was built for his convenience but which, because of his tragic death, he never actually used. Miyagi died in June 1956, at the age of 62, after apparently falling from an express train while on his way to Osaka for a concert.

The museum should appeal both to people interested in Japanese music and to those interested in Miyagi himself. Admission is ¥400 (¥300 for high school students, ¥200 for primary school pupils), and the museum is closed on the second, fourth and fifth Sundays, Mondays, Tuesdays and national holidays.

The memorial hall is located at 35, Nakamachi, Shinjuku Ward, a 10-minute walk from Kagurazaka Station on the Tozai subway line or Iidabashi Station on the JNR Sobu Line. Tel. 03-269-0208.

Imagination Flies on Tail of Kite

Kite Museum   凧の博物館

Nobody knows where or when kites originated. The West claims the fame, as it does with most other inventions of import, by attributing it to the Greek Archytas, while the East says that kites were first flown in China by a general called Han Sin. Whichever may be true, both theories suggest that kites first appeared around 300-200 years B.C., and were used for practical rather than amusement purposes.

Kites first came to Japan from China some time before the start of the Heian Period, and although there must have been early associations with religion, there are apparently records of kites being used for amusement in the early 17th century. It was about that time that kite flying became very popular, and indeed, in 1655 the Tokugawa shogunate actually issued orders banning the pastime because of the congestion it was causing. The enthusiasm of the people won, however, and kite flying continued.

Judging by old prints, early kites in Japan were small and of various designs. In the 19th century, however, kite flying became established as an attraction of the New Year festivities and other festivals. Kite fights and kite-flying tournaments are held all over the country at various times of the year, perhaps the most famous being those at Hamamatsu, Shizuoka, in early May, and at Shirone, Niigata, in June. Often these meetings involve huge kites, the flying of which requires considerable teamwork.

Kites have been made for various reasons: for religious purposes, to keep evil spirits away, to help bring about a good harvest, to celebrate some event or other. A collection of them is on display at the Kite Museum in Nihonbashi, Tokyo. This very bright museum was opened in November 1977 by Shingo Motegi, the founder of the Taimeiken restaurant.

Motegi, who died in 1978, traveled around the world studying cooking and in the process gathered together a very impressive collection of kites, which he then put on display to form this museum.

Altogether Motegi collected over 1,000 kites, and about 200 of them are on display in the museum, the exhibits being changed every three months to allow the other kites to be shown. One of the outstanding kites is the one presented to Motegi by Malaysia, a large and elaborately designed kite. There are also kites from Thailand, China, India, Sri Lanka and Korea, and from all over Japan, from Okinawa to Hokkaido.

Particularly notable among the Japanese kites are those designed after birds, insects and Kabuki. There are swallow kites, horsefly kites, a butterfly streamer kite, and there is also a kite made in 1976 in the shape of a sailing boat. The colors are wonderful, and some of the kites have really excellent drawings on them, especially the large square Edo kites.

The museum is open from 11 a.m. until 4 p.m. and closed on Sundays and national holidays. Entrance is ¥100 for adults and ¥30 for children.

The Kite Museum is located on the fifth floor above the Taimeiken restaurant in Nihonbashi. From Nihonbashi Subway Station, walk toward Edobashi Station and turn left where Tokyu Department Store ends. Taimeiken is a few meters down the road on the right.

Time-Tunnel Trip to Clock Museum

Daimyo Clock Museum　　　　　　　　大名時計博物館

Japanese clocks are more than just clocks made in Japan. *Wadokei,* as they are called, were craft instruments manufactured by hand in the Edo Period for the *daimyo* lords who ordered them and were made to fit the method of telling time in Japan in that period, rather than the now standard 24-hour system which wasn't adopted in this country until into the Meiji Period.

The first foreign-made clock to be brought to Japan is said to have arrived in 1551, and the oldest such clock still in existence came from Mexico in 1611, a present to Tokugawa Ieyasu. It is now in Shizuoka Prefecture. These clocks were of no use to the Japanese, who divided the day not into 24 hourly units, but into two parts of six units each, from daybreak to nightfall and from nightfall to daybreak.

The *daimyo* lords, however, apparently became fascinated by the idea of having clocks, and upon their orders the country's clockmakers, graduates of the missionary schools where they learned their trade, set about making the first *wadokei,* in some cases remodeling the foreign clocks themselves to suit Japanese time. Such remodeled clocks were called *wamae-dokei,* and some of these, together with other Japanese clocks of the Edo Period, are on display at the Daimyo Clock Museum in Tokyo's Taito Ward.

The collection is on show in a special one-room exhibition hall located in the garden of a private house. The only sound in the quiet room is the steady ticking of a clock, while displayed on *tatami* mats in glass cases are several types of *wadokei* from the majestic *yagura-dokei* to the decorative *makura* (pillow)-*dokei,* and the *shaku-dokei,* looking more like a thermometer than a clock with its readings going from top to bottom. There is also an example of a *koban-dokei,* which measured time by the burning of incense sticks.

The *yagura-dokei* is said to have been the oldest of Japanese mechanical clocks and is usually mounted on a pyramid-shaped stand, making it look a fine piece of furniture in itself. It is said to have been developed from early European lantern clocks, although to touch on a small controversy, some scholars do claim that Japanese clocks had a history of their own going back before the introduction of clocks from the West.

Museums are often called time-tunnels, but for none can this description be more appropriate than it is for the clock museum. A sofa and chairs are provided so that visitors can for a short moment at least forget about that next appointment. Indeed, it is not just clocks that are on display here, but a whole way of life in a period when people went to bed when it got dark and got up with the sun, and weren't constantly glancing at their watches.

This does not, however, prevent the museum having its own time schedule. It is closed on Mondays, from Dec. 25 to Jan. 15, and during the summer months of July, August and September. Opening hours are from 10 a.m. to 4 p.m.; if the door is locked, ask at the house and they will open up for you. Entrance is ¥300 for adults, ¥200 for high school students and ¥100 for children.

To reach the Clock Museum, take the exit for Nezu Shrine from Nezu Station on the Chiyoda subway line. Walk along Shinobazu Dori Av. toward Sendagi and cross the road at the first traffic lights after the police box. From here a narrow road leads north up a hill, and the museum is situated just to the left at the top of the hill.

The People's Museum in Ueno

Shitamachi Museum　　　　　　　　　　　下町風俗資料館

Walking into the Shitamachi Museum is like entering one of the many back alleys which still exist in some parts of "downtown" Tokyo. Most museums feature aspects of upper class life through the ages, but this one is devoted to the life of the common people in the 19th and early 20th centuries.

Two back-to-back tenement houses occupy the first floor. In one corner a candy store with various sweets, drinks and trinkets has been recreated, a place where children in the area would have gathered. Visitors are free to pick up and examine the many objects on display, and even the washing has been left out in the passageway around the tenements to create a lived-in atmosphere.

The narrow passageway leads round to a tinsmith's, and recreated opposite the tenement houses is a merchant's house, outside which stands a jinrikisha. The merchant deals in clog throngs, straps which apparently became fashionable after the Meiji Restoration among young *shitamachi* women who enjoyed matching them with their kimonos.

The objects of daily use exhibited in the rooms of these houses were almost all contributed by people living in the *shitamachi* area in Tokyo's Taito Ward and delight both young and old alike. The latter in particular can be seen enthusiastically pointing to furniture here and implements there with cries of "Ah, we had one of these as well!" and "This takes me back!"

The downtown atmosphere continues even on the stairs up to the second floor, with recordings of various street vendor cries played, while the exhibition upstairs shows various aspects of *shitamachi* life from the Edo Period, such as children's games, firefighting equipment, women's combs and teeth-blackening utensils and scenes of Sumida River fireworks displays. Video equipment is also available offering short descriptions of *shitamachi* traditions and crafts which live on.

What was *shitamachi*? Although the 1923 earthquake and World War II bombings erased most of the buildings, this museum, opened in October 1980, tries to provide some clues, recreating the community spirit and closeness of the common people of the area. It is open from 9:30 a.m. to 4:30 p.m., closed on Mondays and national holidays, and admission is ¥200 for adults and ¥100 for children.

Shitamachi Museum

The Shitamachi Museum is located in a corner of Ueno Park, a short walk from JNR Ueno Station and near Keisei Ueno Station.

Records of Yokohama's Past

Yokohama Archives 横浜開港資料館

When Commodore Perry brought his squadron of four black ships to Japan in 1853, delivering a letter from the American president to the Japanese emperor calling for the opening of the secluded empire, it marked the beginning of a two-way process. If Japan was to start learning from foreign countries, so also was the West to begin learning about Japan.

The Illustrated London News wrote of the coming event on May 7, 1853: "So the expedition goes to coerce the Government of Japan into civilization, and if she will not consent to negotiate with a nation whose subjects she has treated with barbarity (referring to the Japanese treatment of shipwrecked foreign sailors), she is to be taught a lesson of humanity and be made to wheel into the ranks of civilized empires."

This article is one of the many exhibits on display at the Yokohama Archives of History Museum, which opened in June 1981, aimed at preserving and exhibiting documents, photographs, books, prints, models and chinaware relating to the history of the port city from the end of the Tokugawa shogunate to the end of the Taisho Period (1912-26).

The museum is located on the site of the former British Consulate, in the area where the Japan-U.S. Treaty of Peace and Amity was signed in 1854. Indeed, in the courtyard of the museum is a large camphor tree under which it is said the treaty was signed. The roots of the tree survived the great earthquake of 1923 and were transplanted to where it now stands.

The first exhibition room deals with "Newborn Yokohama: Japan's Encounter with the West." Through various prints, maps and models, including one of James Watt's steam engine, the opening up of port and country are put in historical perspective. Among the exhibits which catch the eye are the old books, one the "Narrative of the Expedition of an American Squadron to the China Seas and Japan 1856-58," in which the following is written of a visit to a town in Japan:

"The wife and sister of the town official soon entered with refreshments and smiled a timid welcome to the visitors. These women were barefooted and bare legged, and were dressed very nearly alike, in dark colored robes, with much of the undress look of night gowns secured by a broad band passing round the waist."

The second exhibition room covers "Blooming Yokohama: Its Early Days of Modernization," with references to the growth of the small village of Yokohama into a large port, the emergence of the foreign settlement, the development of the silk trade and so on. A third room is devoted to special exhibitions, while the consulate building across the courtyard remains with a memorial hall.

On visiting the archives, one notes with interest Commodore Perry's prophecy, that "Once possessed of the acquisitions of the past and present of the civilized world, the Japanese would enter as powerful competitors in the race for mechanical success in the future."

The museum is closed on Mondays and the day following a national holiday. It is open from 9:30 a.m. to 4:30 p.m., and entrance is ¥200 for adults and ¥100 for children. A reading room is also open to the public.

The Yokohama Archives is located near the Silk Center, about a 10-minute walk from JNR Kannai Station.

LIST OF MUSEUMS

A full list of exhibitions at main museums and art galleries in and around Tokyo appears regularly in the English-language press. The following is a list of less well-known museums in the area.

Museum of Maritime Science —an educational museum stressing the present and the future more than the past. In Kaijo Park, Koto Ward. Take bus from Monzennakacho Station on Tozai subway line or boat from Takeshiba Wharf, near JNR Hamamatsucho Station. Tel. 03-528-1111.

Tobacco and Salt Museum — an unlikely but fascinating combination. Located in Shibuya Ward. Closed Mondays and national holidays. Tel. 03-476-2041.

NHK Broadcasting Museum — an introduction to a modern culture. In Minato Ward, from Kamiyacho Station on the Hibiya subway line. Closed Mondays. Tel. 03-433-5211.

Sugino Gakuen Costume Museum — fashions from East and West. In Osaki, Shinagawa Ward, from JNR Meguro Station. Closed Mondays, national holidays and school holidays. Tel. 03-491-8151.

Meiji University Penal Museum — implements of punishment from the Edo Period and after. In Chiyoda Ward, from JNR Ochanomizu Station. Closed Sundays, national holidays and school holidays. Tel. 03-296-4431.

Sword Museum — about 40 swords on display at a time. From Sangubashi Station on the Odakyu Line from Shinjuku. Closed on Mondays. Tel. 03-379-1386.

Chihiro Iwasaki Picture Book Museum — many delights, especially for children. In Nerima Ward, from Kami Igusa Station on the Seibu Shinjuku Line. Closed Tuesdays and Wednesdays, unless these days are national holidays. Tel. 03-995-0612.

Waseda University Tsubouchi Memorial Theater Museum — sets and costumes from Shakespeare to Kabuki, and various prints, masks and so on. By bus from JNR Takadanobaba Station or from Waseda Station on Tozai subway line. Closed Mondays and national holidays. Tel. 03-203-4141.

Nihon Mingeikan — an excellent collection of Japanese folk crafts. In Meguro Ward, from Komaba Todaimae Station on the Inokashira Line. Closed on Mondays. Tel. 03-467-4527.

Transport Museum — everything from the palanquin to the Shinkansen and beyond. Near JNR Akihabara Station. Closed on Mondays. Tel. 03-251-8481.

Goto Planetarium and Astronautical Museum — Japan's first planetarium, opened in 1957. On the 8th fl. of the Tokyu Bunka Kaikan, opposite JNR Shibuya Station. Closed on Mondays. Tel. 03-407-7409.

Communications Museum — a short history, but a big future. A short walk from Otemachi Subway Station, or from JNR Tokyo Station. Closed Mondays. Tel. 03-270-3841.

Furniture Museum— particularly interesting for its displays of old chests and chairs. Closed on Sundays and national holidays. Near Harumi Post Office bus stop. Tel. 03-533-0098.

Meguro Parasite Museum — for a look at some of our less welcome guests. From JNR Meguro Station. Closed Mondays and national holidays. Tel. 03-716-1264.

Tokyo From Above

Shinjuku's skyscrapers as viewed from a light plane

The Capital's High Spots

Skyscrapers 高層ビル

The elevators make the ascent seem so easy, and indeed, as Tokyo's skyscrapers have got higher and higher, so elevators have got faster and faster.

Tokyo's highest building, Sunshine 60 in Ikebukuro, has what is said to be the fastest elevator in the world. It gets you up to the top at a speed of 600 meters per minute. Sunshine 60 stands 226.2 meters high, which means that you can shoot up to the top floor in 22.62 seconds. That is to say, if the same elevator were used to reach the summit of Mount Fuji — 3,776 meters — then that climb would take just 6.3 minutes.

One of the main purposes of going up is to look down, and the whole of the top floor of Sunshine 60 is an observatory, with a variety of sidelights including a coffee shop, game corner, computer fortune-telling, a copy service for the newspaper of the day on which you were born and so on, extras which seem to thrive at all observation platforms in Japan. There are a number of other attractions in Sunshine 60 as well, including a planetarium and an aquarium.

Most people, however, will be attracted more by the view than the sidelights. In this respect, Sunshine 60's observatory is a bit on the expensive side — ¥500 — and the high spots of Shinjuku provide the best offers. The Shinjuku Center Building, Sumitomo and Nomura buildings all have observatories which are free, on the 53rd, 51st and 50th floors respectively.

The first of the Shinjuku buildings to go up after the plan to create a Tokyo subcenter in the area was announced in 1960 was the Keio Plaza Hotel, construction of which was completed in 1971, followed in 1974 by the KDD, Mitsui and Sumitomo buildings, the latter being the famous triangular *sankaku biru*.

In 1976 came the Yasuda Building, in 1978 the Shinjuku Center Building, which for those who get caught in the rain is conveniently connected underground with the west exit of Shinjuku Station. Added to the cluster more recently have been the Century Hyatt Hotel, Daiichi Seimei Building, and the Keio Plaza Hotel South Annex.

The highest building in Shinjuku is the Center Building, which is the brownish one in the middle standing 223 meters high, with 54 floors up and four floors down. Also over 200 meters are the Mitsui Building (210 meters, 55 floors), the Nomura Building (204 meters, 53 floors) and Sumitomo Building, which scrapes into the group at 200 meters and 52 floors.

All of these buildings make up independent communities in themselves, with an endless number of offices, shops and restaurants filling their floors, and an appeal definitely aimed at the young fashionable set, such as the Nomura Building's Pair Town of fashion boutiques and eating places. It is said, by the way, that some 10,000 people work in the Shinjuku Center Building alone.

For those interested in the views from these high spots, winter and early spring are probably the best times of the year. Try and choose a day with a clear blue sky, if possible after it has rained, and with a strong wind to blow all the smog away.

On a very good day, the view should extend from Mount Fuji across to the Chichibu hills. Looking out to the southwest from Shinjuku you should be able to make out, together with Mount Fuji, the Tanzawa and Oyama mountains, and Mount Takao should be visible in the foreground. To the northwest, look out for Bukozan, Kumotoriyama and, nearer at hand, Mount Mitake.

The Mitsui Building, by the way, has no observatory and the KDD building is not open to the public. The Keio Plaza Hotel has a coffee lounge observatory, although it is also possible just to go for the view, and the Yasuda Building has an observatory in an art gallery with an entrance fee of ¥300. The Togo Gallery is on the

42nd floor and looks to the east, that is, into Tokyo itself. It is open only from 9:30 a.m. to 4:30 p.m., which means that night views cannot be had from there.

The other buildings are open until later, with the Center Building allowing a view until 11 p.m. Good views can also be had by dining in the various restaurants located on the upper floors of the buildings.

Of course, the high spots of Tokyo do not end in Ikebukuro and Shinjuku. The Kasumigaseki Building has an observatory on its 36th floor, and Tokyo Tower, which at 333 meters stands 11 meters higher than the Eiffel Tower in Paris, has observation platforms at 150 meters and 250 meters, as well as various other attractions, including a waxworks.

Down the road from Tokyo Tower is the World Trade Center Building in Hamamatsucho, which has an observatory on its 40th floor, open from 10 a.m. to 8:30 p.m., with an entrance fee of ¥400. Immediately below can be seen Hama Rikyu Garden, and a particularly good view is had of Tokyo Bay.

To Tokyo Tower and Back — by Air

Light Plane   本田飛行場

"Just aim straight for Shinjuku," the pilot said casually, and turned to point out the Arakawa River to the other two passengers in the Cessna 172.

The single-engined Cessna, as snug-fitting as a sports car, flies out of Honda Airport in Saitama Prefecture, which offers more than 20 sightseeing courses over Tokyo and the surrounding countryside and gives a novice in the front passenger seat a chance at the controls.

Trips range from a quick ride to nearby Okegawa City, further afield to Tobu Zoo and the UNESCO Village, a flight right over central Tokyo (or in the opposite direction as far as Nagatoro), and longest and most expensive of all, down to Kamakura and Enoshima, which would cost three people over ¥50,000.

One of the most popular courses is to Tokyo Tower and back, enabling passengers flying at an altitude of 2,000 feet at 100 mph to pick out many of the sprawling city's landmarks.

Highlights include flying directly over the Nishi-Shinjuku skyscrapers and the rare opportunity to see over the walls of the Imperial Palace.

Circling Tokyo Tower affords an excellent view of Tokyo Bay and downtown, and on the homeward stretch there's a chance to catch up with the baseball when passing directly over Korakuen Stadium.

Tokyo's several parks and gardens are welcome patches of green amid the traffic jam of predominantly double-decker housing below, including Shinjuku Gyoen, the Meiji Shrine Inner Garden, Tokyo University Botanical Gardens and Rikugien, not to mention the extensive grounds of the Imperial Palace.

Honda Airport itself is marked from the air by its green surroundings. It sits in a long meadow by the banks of the Arakawa River — the walk there is beautiful — and the meadow is visible several minutes before the plane begins its descent. After a gentle landing, the Cessna rolls to a halt and deposits passengers to one side of the small runway.

It takes about two hours to reach Honda Airport from the center of Tokyo by conventional means, and the Cessna covers the distance there and back in 35 minutes.

The Tokyo Tower course costs three people ¥27,300. A larger plane (one pilot and five passengers) completes the same course in slightly less time (32 minutes) for ¥35,500. The airport operates sightseeing flights between 9 a.m. and 4 p.m. daily. For further information, and to reserve flights, telephone Honda Airport at 0492-97-2044.

To get to Honda Airport, take the Tobu Tojo Line from Ikebukuro to Kawagoe (an express stop), then transfer to bus No. 4 bound for Okegawa Station, alighting at Yamagayato. Follow the bus up the hill, turning right onto a cycle path running parallel with the Arakawa River. The airfield is a 15-minute walk away, and the airport office is on the right.

Calendar

In the precincts of Meiji Shrine at New Year's

Month by Month

The following is a calendar list of festivals and events held in and around Tokyo throughout the year. Please remember that dates and times are subject to change. For further information on these and other events, contact the Japan National Tourist Organization in Tokyo (tel.: 502-1461).

JANUARY

Shrines and temples are crowded over the first few days of the New Year as Japan celebrates its most important holiday. Tokyo's Meiji Shrine attracts tens of thousands from midnight on. It is a good time to see Mt. Fuji from the city because roads are less congested and the air much clearer as a result.

Jan. 1: *Ganjitsu,* or New Year's Day Holiday

Jan. 1-3: New Year ceremonies and entertainments at Yasukuni Shrine, including Noh, Japanese dance and music. Nearest station: Kudanshita on Tozai subway line.

Jan. 2: *Ippan Sanga,* the New Year congratulatory visit to the Imperial Palace. The palace grounds are opened and the public invited to pay its respects to the imperial family, who appear on a balcony several times during the day.

Jan. 6: *Dezome Shiki,* the first review of the year of the Tokyo Metropolitan Fire Brigade. The event features a mixture of modern fire-fighting equipment and thrilling acrobatics by firemen dressed in the costume of the old Edo Fire Brigade. Near Harumi Pier, from 10 to 11.30 a.m.

Jan. 8: *Dondo Yaki.* Used New Year's decorations are burnt at Torigoe Shrine in Asakusa. Nearest station: Asakusa on Ginza or Toei Asakusa subway lines.

Jan. 12: *Daruma Ichi,* a fair of daruma dolls. Hundreds of stalls selling daruma dolls, food and other items are set up along Ome Kaido Avenue in Ome City, Saitama Pref. Nearest station: Ome on JNR Ome Line.

Jan. 15: *Momote Shiki,* an archery ritual to commemorate *Seijin-no-Hi* (Adulthood Day) in the precincts of Meiji Jingu Shrine, from 1 to 3 p.m. Nearest station: Harajuku on Yamanote Line or Meijijingumae on Chiyoda subway line.

Jan. 15 & 16: *Boro Ichi,* which literally means "rag fair," on Daikan-Yashikimae Dori Avenue, Kamimachi, Setagaya Ward, featuring about 700 roadside vendors selling everything from food to old agricultural implements — but no rags. Take bus 1, 3 or 34 from Shibuya Station south exit, alighting at Kamimachi bus stop.

FEBRUARY

February is the month of *Setsubun,* the bean-throwing ceremony that marks the end of winter and the beginning of spring. It's also a chance to watch priests splash cold water on each other in ascetic ritual.

Feb. 3 (or thereabouts): *Setsubun* (bean-throwing ceremony) at noted shrines and temples around Japan. The bean-throwing is accompanied by shouts of "Out, devils! In, good luck!" to ensure good fortune for the coming year. In Tokyo, noted personalities help scatter the beans at Asakusa Kannon Temple (Asakusa on the Ginza or Toei Asakusa subway lines), Zojoji Temple (Onarimon on the Toei Mita subway line), Ikegami Hommonji Temple (Ikegami on the Ikegami Line) and Kanda Myojin Shrine (Ochanomizu on the Sobu Line).

141

Feb. 8: *Hari-kuyo,* a service for broken pins and needles held at Shojuin Temple, Shinjuku Ward. Nearest station: Shinjuku Gyoen-mae on the Marunouchi subway line.

Feb. 12: *Ara-gyo,* an ascetic exercise at Choshoji Temple in Kamakura during which a group of Buddhist priests in loin cloths splash cold water over themselves while chanting sutra.

Feb. 15: *Suigyo Kokutoe,* a cold water ablution practised by priests at Nose Myokenzan Betsuin Temple, Sumida Ward, from 1 p.m. Nearest station: Kinshicho Station on the Sobu Line, and then by bus.

Tako Ichi, or kite fairs, are held at Oji Inari Shrine, Kishi-machi, Kita Ward, two or three times during the month. Nearest station: Oji on Keihin Tohoku Line.

MARCH

The annual Peach Blossom Festival, also known as *Hina Matsuri* (doll festival) or girls' festival, is the major celebration held throughout the country in March, centering on the third day of the month. Featured in this special ceremony for girls is a set of *"hina"* dolls and miniature household articles arranged on a tier of shelves covered with bright red cloth.

March 3 & 4: *Daruma Ichi,* a daruma doll fair at Jindaiji Temple, Chofu City, on the outskirts of Tokyo. Several hundred stalls are set up along the temple approaches and in the temple compound from 10 a.m. to 4 p.m. Nearest station: Tsutsujigaoka on the Keio Line.

March 9: *Hiwatari,* a fire-walking ceremony held at Yakuoin Temple on Mt. Takao. *Yamabushi* (mountain priests) walk barefoot across the still-flickering embers of a bonfire. Nearest station: Takaosanguchi on the Keio Line.

March 18: *Kinryu-no-mai,* a Golden Dragon Dance, in the precincts of the Asakusa Kannon Temple. The dance, which lasts about 10 minutes, is performed twice in the day. Nearest station: Asakusa on Ginza or Toei Asakusa subway lines.

APRIL

April is the time of year for cherry blossom viewing in Tokyo, at such parks as Inokashira (near Kichijoji Station on Chuo Line), Asukayama (Oji Station on Keihin Tohoku Line) and Ueno (Ueno Station on Yamanote Line). It is also the month of Buddha's birthday — April 8 — celebrated at all Buddhist temples by the *Hana Matsuri,* a floral festival.

Early April: Akabane *Baka Matsuri,* the festival of April Fool's Day. Nearest station: Akabane on Keihin Tohoku Line.

April 8: *Hana Matsuri.* A small image of Buddha is displayed at Buddhist temples and sweet tea *(amacha)* is poured over it as an expression of devotion. Children parade behind a replica of a white elephant, a sacred animal associated with Buddha.

April 21-23: The Spring Festival of Yasukuni Shrine. A number of events, including *kobudo* (ancient martial arts), Japanese dance and folk singing are held at the Nohgakudo Stage near the main hall of worship. Nearest station: Kudanshita on Tozai subway line.

Late April-Early May: The Spring Festival of Meiji Shrine, including *kagura* (sacred Shinto music and dance), Noh, *sankyoku (koto, shamisen* and *shakuhachi* music) and archery. Nearest station: Harajuku on Yamanote Line or Meijijingumae on Chiyoda subway line.

Mid-April: Kamakura *Matsuri,* the festival of the Tsurugaoka Hachimangu Shrine in Kamakura, featuring events such as sacred dance and horseback archery. Nearest station: Kamakura on JNR Yokosuka Line.

MAY

This month sees one of Tokyo's biggest festivals, the *Sanja Matsuri* in Asakusa. *Kodomo-no-Hi* (Children's Day) is celebrated on May 5.

Late April-Early May: Spring Festival of Meiji Shrine (see April)

May 3 & 5: *Otako-age,* giant kite flying near Zakkaibashi Bridge, Zama City, Kanagawa Pref., from 9 a.m. to 4 p.m. Nearest station: Zama on Odakyu Line.

May 3-5: *Oshiro Matsuri,* a castle festival at Odawara City in Kanagawa Pref. Highlight is a procession of people in feudal costume in the precincts of Odawara Castle. Nearest station: Odawara on Odakyu Line or Tokaido Line.

May 4 & 5: *Otako-age,* giant kite flying on the dry bed of the Sagami River, at Isobe, Sagamihara, from 10 a.m. to 5 p.m. Dozens of men try to fly a kite weighing 800 kg. Nearest station: Sagamihara on Odakyu Line.

Mid-May: Kanda *Matsuri,* the festival of the Kanda Myojin Shrine, featuring processions of small and large *mikoshi* (portable shrines). Nearest stations: Ochanomizu on Chuo/Sobu lines and Marunouchi subway line, or Shin-Ochanomizu on Chiyoda subway line.

May 16-18: *Sanja Matsuri,* the festival of Asakusa Shrine. The main event is a parade of 1000 people in traditional attire, including *geisha* playing *Sanja bayashi* music. *Mikoshi* fill the streets. Nearest station: Asakusa on Ginza or Toei Asakusa subway lines.

May 31: *Ueki Ichi,* a potted plant fair in the neighborhood of Sengen Shrine, Asakusa. Nearest station: Asakusa on Ginza or Toei Asakusa subway lines.

JUNE

Iris flowers are at their best in the middle of June, and here are some good places to see them (nearest stations in brackets): Meiji Shrine Garden (Harajuku on Yamanote Line, or Meijijingumae on Chiyoda subway line); Yasukuni Shrine (Kudanshita on Tozai subway line); Keio Hyakkaen (Keio Tamagawaen on Keio Sagamihara Line from Chofu); Mizumoto Park (by bus from Kanamachi on Joban Line); Horikiri Shobuen (Horikiri Shobuen on Keisei Line); and Jindai Shokubutsuen (by bus from Tsutsujigaoka Station on Keio Line).

June 1 & 30: *Ueki Ichi,* a potted plant fair on the streets around Sengen Shrine, Asakusa. Nearest station: Asakusa on Ginza or Toei Asakusa subway lines.

Early June: Annual festival of Torigoe Shrine. About 70 *mikoshi* (portable shrines), including the biggest in Tokyo, are paraded about the neighborhood.

June 10-16: *Sanno Matsuri,* the annual festival of Hie Shrine in Akasaka, including tea ceremony and folk dancing. Nearest stations: Akasaka on Chiyoda subway line, and Akasaka Mitsuke on Ginza or Marunouchi subway lines.

June 30-July 2: *The Fuji Matsuri,* the annual festival to mark the opening of Mt. Fuji to climbers, held at Fuji Shrine. Nearest station: Komagome on Yamanote Line.

JULY

Mid-July is the time of *O-Bon,* a Festival of Souls, when Buddhist families welcome back deceased relatives on a brief visit from the spirit world.

July 1: *Ueki Ichi,* a potted plant fair on the streets around Sengen Temple in Asakusa. Nearest station: Asakusa on Ginza or Toei Asakusa subway lines.

July 6-8: *Asagao Ichi,* a morning glory fair, held in the precincts of Kishibojin Temple. The fair is open from 5 a.m. to midnight daily. Nearest station: Iriya on Hibiya subway line.

July 9 &10: *Hozuki Ichi,* a ground cherry fair in the precincts of the Asakusa Kannon Temple. Hundreds of street stalls are set up selling ground cherries and windbells. Nearest station: Asakusa on Ginza or Toei Asakusa subway lines.

July 13-16: *Mitama Matsuri,* a festival of souls held at Yasukuni Shrine and featuring *Bon Odori* folk dancing, classical dance, a parade of *mikoshi* and an exhibition of famous lanterns from all over Japan.

Mid-July to Mid-August: *Edo-shumi Noryo Taikai,* or Summer Evening Festival, on the shores of Shinobazu Pond and in the compound of the pagoda in Ueno Park. On July 17, from 7 p.m., lighted lanterns are set afloat on waters of the pond. Nearest station: Ueno on Yamanote/Keihin Tohoku lines or Ginza subway line.

July 19 & 20: *Kawase-Sai* Festival at Chichibu Shrine, Chichibu in Saitama Pref., including parades of floats and *mikoshi,* and *mikoshi* being borne into the Arakawa River.

July 20: *Hanabi Taikai,* a fireworks display in Yamashita Park in Yokohama, from 6:30 p.m. to 8:30 p.m. Nearest station: Kannai on Keihin Tohoku Line.

Late July: *Hanabi Taikai* on the Edo River near Shibamata Ground, from 7:30 p.m. to 9 p.m. Nearest station: Kanamachi on Joban Line.

AUGUST

Despite the sticky weather, there's still plenty going on in August.

Aug. 4-6: *Setomono Ichi,* a ceramics fair held on Shin-Ohashi Dori near Suitengu Shrine. Nearest station: Ningyocho on Hibiya subway line.

Aug. 4-6: *Mitama Matsuri,* a festival of souls held at Ikegami Hommonji Temple. Children carrying lighted lanterns parade around the temple and *Bon Odori* folk dances are performed. Nearest station: Ikegami on Ikegami Line.

Aug. 6-10: *Tanabata Matsuri* (star festival) is held along the Asagaya Shopping Street, which is bedecked in streamers and decorations. Nearest station: Asagaya on Chuo Line.

Aug. 13-15: Annual festival of the Tomioka Hachimangu Shrine, featuring dance, music, flower arrangement and *kendo* displays. Nearest station: Monzennakacho on Tozai subway line.

Aug. 26-28: *Awa Odori.* This folk dance, native to Tokushima Prefecture on Shikoku, is enthusiastically performed in the streets of

Koenji from 6:30 p.m. to 9:30 p.m. daily. Nearest station: Koenji on Chuo Line.

SEPTEMBER

Hot summer days are almost over, and Sept. 23 (or 24) is autumn equinox day, a national holiday. Typhoons may place longer trips in doubt, but it's a good time to enjoy local travel and local festivals.

Sept. 12 & 13: The festival of Nogi Shrine, which sees the residence of the late Gen. Nogi of Russo-Japanese War fame open to the public from 10 a.m. to 4 p.m. on both days, and recitation of Chinese poems and a sword dance performed about 4:30 p.m. on Oct. 13. Nearest station: Nogizaka on Chiyoda subway line.

Sept. 13-15: Festival of Anahachiman Shrine, with a parade of *mikoshi* and *Bon Odori* folk dances. Nearest station: Waseda on Tozai subway line.

Sept. 14-16: *Dara-Dara Matsuri* festival of Shiba Dai-Jingu Shrine, Minato Ward, featuring a parade of portable shrines on Sept. 14. Nearest station: Hamamatsucho on Yamanote Line, or Daimon on Toei Asakusa Line.

Sept. 14-16: Tsurugaoka Hachimangu Festival in Kamakura, made up of a series of pageants and displays of martial contests. Kamakura-*bayashi* music is played all day on Sept. 14, on Sept. 15 there is a *mikoshi* parade from 1 to 3 p.m. and *kyudo*, kendo and judo meets, and on Sept. 16 *yabusame* (horseback archery), followed by dances and festival music. Nearest station: Kamakura on JNR Yokosuka Line.

Sept. 25: *Ningyo Kuyo,* a mass to comfort the souls of dolls no longer wanted, held from 2 p.m. at Kiyomizu Kannon temple in Ueno Park. Nearest station: Ueno on Yamanote Line.

Sept. 26-28: Festival of Kaichu Inari Shrine in Hyakunincho, Shinjuku Ward, featuring a procession of *mikoshi.* Every other year there is a parade of musketeers.

OCTOBER

Several attractive lantern-lit processions take place around the city this month, and two major shrines hold their autumn festivals.

Oct. 1: Festival of the Igusa Hachiman Shrine, Suginami Ward, featuring *kagura* (Shinto music and dance), flower arrangement exhibitions and demonstrations of *kendo*. Nearest station: Ogikubo on Chuo Line, and then by bus.

Oct. 10: *Kusajishi-Shiki* at Yasukuni Shrine. A group of archers dressed in ceremonial white robes shoot at a target — a picture of a deer. Nearest station: Kudanshita on Tozai subway line.

Oct. 10: *Yabusame* (horseback archery) at Toyama Park by Anahachiman Shrine. Nearest station: Waseda on Tozai subway line.

Oct 11-13: *O-eshiki* Festival of Hommonji Temple, Ikegami, Ota Ward, which features a parade of 80 to 100 lanterns of various sizes, decorated with paper cherry blossoms, from 8 p.m. to 11 p.m. on Oct. 12. The ritual is held to commemorate the death of the holy priest Nichiren, who died at this site in 1282.

Oct. 12-13: *O-eshiki* Festival at Myohoji Temple, featuring parade of lanterns from 7 p.m. to 9 p.m. on Oct. 13. Nearest station: Higashi Koenji on Marunouchi subway line.

Oct. 14-15: Kawagoe Festival, in Kawagoe City, Saitama Pref., featuring a parade of gorgeously decorated floats from 10 a.m. to 10 p.m. on Oct. 15. Nearest station: Kawagoe City on Tobu Tojo Line.

October 16-18: Festival of Kishibojin Temple, Zoshigaya, featuring a parade of lighted lanterns from 7 p.m. to 9 p.m. from Gokokuji Temple to Kishibojin Temple on Oct. 17 and from 7:30 p.m. to 9:30 p.m. from the park in front of Seibu Department Store to Kishibojin Temple on Oct. 18. Nearest station: Mejiro on Yamanote Line.

Oct. 16-Nov. 15: Chrysanthemum exhibition at Yasukuni Shrine. Nearest station: Kudanshita on Tozai subway line.

Oct. 17-19: Annual Autumn Festival of Yasukuni Shrine,

148

featuring Japanese dance, folk songs, Noh, martial arts, from 10 a.m. to 6 p.m.

Oct. 18: *Kinryu-no-Mai,* a golden dragon dance in the compound of Asakusa Kannon Temple. Nearest station: Asakusa on Ginza subway line.

Oct. 25-Nov. 23: Chrysanthemum exhibition at Meiji Shrine. Nearest station: Harajuku on Yamanote Line, or Meijijingumae on Chiyoda subway line.

Oct. 30-Nov. 4: Annual autumn festival of Meiji Shrine featuring Noh plays, Japanese music and dance, *bugaku* (old court music) and various martial arts. Nearest station: Harajuku on Yamanote Line, or Meijijingumae on Chiyoda subway line.

NOVEMBER

Autumn is the season for chrysanthemums, Japan's national flower, and November is a good month to view them. Chrysanthemum exhibitions are held at the following places in Tokyo (nearest stations in brackets): Yasukuni Shrine (Kudanshita on Tozai subway line), Sensoji Temple (Asakusa on Ginza subway line), Meiji Shrine (Harajuku on Yamanote Line, or Meijijingumae on Chiyoda subway line), Shinjuku Gyoen National Garden (Shinjuku Gyoenmae on Marunouchi subway line), Hibiya Park (Hibiya on Hibiya subway line), Jindaiji Botanical Garden (Tsutsujigaoka on Keio Line, then by bus).

Nov. 1-30: *Momiji Matsuri,* a maple festival centering on Yakuoin Temple, on Mt. Takao. Nearest station: Takaosanguchi on Keio Line.

Nov. 3: *Shirasagi-no-Mai,* a white heron dance in the precincts of Asakusa Kannon Temple, at 11.30 a.m. and 3.30 p.m. Nearest station: Asakusa on Ginza subway line.

Nov. 6: *Hiwatari,* a fire walking ceremony at Akiba Shrine, Matsugaya, Taito Ward, from 5 p.m. Nearest station: Inaricho on Ginza subway line.

Nov. 15: *Shichi-Go-San,* or seven-five-three, the day that girls of seven, boys of five, and girls and boys of three visit shrines to express their thanks for having reached their ages safely, and to pray for continued health and happiness. The most popular shrines in Tokyo for this are Meiji Shrine in Harajuku, Hie Shrine in Akasaka, and Kanda Myojin Shrine in Kanda.

Bird Days: *Tori-no-Ichi* fairs are held at many Otori shrines in Tokyo on Bird Days in November. *Kumade* (ornamental rakes) are sold. The biggest *Tori-no-Ichi* fair in Tokyo is at Otori Shrine in Asakusa. Nearest station: Minowa, on Hibiya subway line.

DECEMBER

The last month of the year is a busy time for everyone, and this is reflected in the number of fairs held in and around Tokyo.

Dec. 3: Chichibu *Yo-Matsuri,* a spectacular night festival held in Chichibu City, Saitama Pref. Two lavishly bedecked carts and four floats assemble at Chichibu Shrine and then proceed through the streets to Chichibu Park.

Dec. 5: *Osame-no-Suitengu* (Year-end Fair) at Suitengu Shrine, Ningyocho, on the Hibiya subway line, from 8 a.m. to 11p.m.

Dec. 6: *Kumade Ichi* at Oji Shrine, Kita Ward, near Oji Station on the JNR Keihin Tohoku Line, from 3 to 10 p.m. *Kumade* are garden rakes decorated with symbols of good luck — such as treasure ships — and are sold at stalls set up in the shrine compound.

Dec. 6: *Hibuse Matsuri* (Fire Festival) at Ryokakuin Temple on Mt. Akiba, Odawara City, Kanagawa Prefecture, from 6 p.m. to 8 p.m.

Dec. 9 & 10: *Seki-no-Ichi* at Honryuji Temple, Sekimachi, Nerima Ward, near Musashiseki Station on the Seibu Shinjuku Line, from 2 to 11 p.m. The fair features many open-air stalls.

Dec. 10: *Toka-Machi* Festival of Hikawa Shrine, Omiya City, Saitama Prefecture. Many open air stalls will be selling *kumade,* daruma dolls and New Year's decorations.

Dec. 14: *Gishi-Sai.* This is the day that the 47 *Ronin* (Loyal Retainers) of Daimyo Asano took their lives in 1702 after avenging the death of their master by killing his enemy. A parade reenacting the famous vendetta starts from Nihon Memmo Co. near Higashi Nihonbashi Station on the Toei Asakusa subway line, crossing Ryogoku Bridge and arriving for a reception at Matsuzakacho Park at 6.30 p.m. The "warriors" then board the subway for Sengakuji Temple, where the loyal 47 are buried, and where a Buddhist Mass is performed.

Dec. 15-28: *Gasa Ichi* at the back of the Asakusa Kannon Temple, near Asakusa Station on the Ginza subway line. About 10 wholesale organizations set up stalls selling New Year's decorations.

Dec. 15 & 16: *Boro Ichi* ("rag fair") on the Daikan-Yashikimae Dori Avenue, Kamimachi, Setagaya Ward. Many stalls will be selling food, potted plants, clothes, old farm implements and other fascinating odds and ends. It is 20 minutes by bus from Shibuya St. south exit: take any bus numbered 1, 2, or 34 and alight at Kamimachi bus stop.

Dec. 17-19: *Hagoita Ichi.* This is a fair selling battledores, in the compound of the Asakusa Kannon Temple (see above).

Dec. 21: *Osame-no-Daishi* (Year-end Fair) at Kawasaki Daishi Temple, Kawasaki City, Kanagawa Pref.

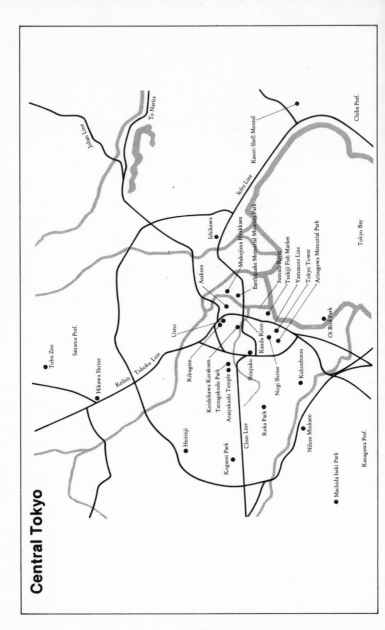

Central Tokyo

- Joban Line
- To Narita
- Kasori Shell Mound
- Chiba Pref.
- Sobu Line
- Ichikawa
- Mukojima Hyakkaen
- Earthquake Memorial Museum Park
- Sumida River
- Tsukiji Fish Market
- Yamanote Line
- Tokyo Tower
- Arisugawa Memorial Park
- Tokyo Bay
- Asakusa
- Oi Bird Park
- Saitama Pref.
- Ueno
- Kanda River
- Tobu Zoo
- Hikawa Shrine
- Keihin Tohoku Line
- Rikugien
- Koishikawa Korakuen
- Tetsugakudo Park
- Araiyakushi Temple
- Shinjuku
- Nogi Shrine
- Kuhonbutsu
- Heirinji
- Roka Park
- Chuo Line
- Nihon Minkaen
- Koganei Park
- Kanagawa Pref.
- Machida Iseki Park

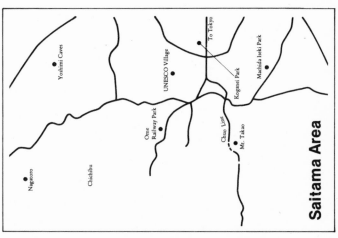

Kanagawa Area

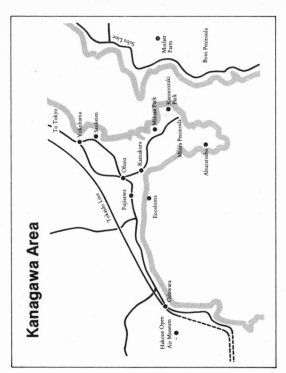

Saitama Area